365 DAYS OF WORLD HISTORY

A Timeline of Daily Lessons from Ancient Empires to Modern Times — With 1000+ Facts and Challenges for Curious Minds

DAE LEE

For our Lou

CONTENTS

PREFACE

In crafting "365 Days of World History," we set out to capture humanity's most remarkable journey - the story of us all. Each daily entry offers a window into our shared past, carefully curated to reveal the surprising connections, unlikely heroes, and pivotal moments that shaped our world. From the first toolmakers of East Africa to the architects of our digital age, these stories remind us that history isn't just about memorizing dates - it's about understanding how we became who we are.

This book represents a collaboration between historians, researchers, and storytellers, all committed to making the complexity of world history accessible without sacrificing its richness. While we've strived for accuracy in every detail, history is always a dialogue between past and present. Any remaining oversights are, of course, our own.

INTRODUCTION

Imagine walking through time with history's greatest figures as your guides. What would Genghis Khan tell you about leadership? What could an ancient Egyptian sculptor teach you about innovation? What wisdom might a Tang Dynasty merchant share about global commerce? "365 Days of World History" offers this journey, providing daily encounters with the remarkable characters, crucial moments, and revolutionary ideas that shaped our world.

History is often presented as a parade of wars, kings, and dates. But the real story of humanity is far richer - it's about how ideas spread, how innovations transformed daily life, and how ordinary people shaped extraordinary events. From the marketplace of ancient Baghdad to the laboratories of Silicon Valley, from the shipyards of Ming China to the assembly lines of Detroit, each daily reading reveals how past human experiences illuminate our present challenges and future possibilities.

Our journey follows humanity's story chronologically, but with a crucial difference - each day highlights surprising connections across time and space. You'll discover how Persian postal systems influenced American democracy, how African metallurgy transformed European warfare, and how Chinese inventions revolutionized Western thinking. These connections reveal history not as isolated events but as an intricate web of human experience.

This book isn't simply about remembering what happened - it's about understanding why it matters. Each daily entry combines vivid storytelling with thought-provoking analysis, asking you to consider how ancient solutions might apply to modern problems. Whether you're curious about how societies handle change, how innovations spread, or how cultures interact, you'll find insights relevant to today's world.

Each daily entry follows a carefully crafted format designed to both inform and intrigue. You'll begin with the historical context - when and where events occurred - followed by a few paragraphs that set the scene and challenge common assumptions. Every page tries to connect these events to broader themes in human development, showing how this moment fits into our larger story. Every entry concludes with a thought-provoking question and four possible answers. These aren't mere tests of memory - they're carefully researched revelations that often surprise even history enthusiasts. The correct answer (provided at the bottom of each page) usually teaches you something unexpected about the day's topic, encouraging deeper reflection on what you've learned.

As you explore these daily histories, approach them with curiosity and imagination. Consider how each story connects to your own experience and understanding of the world. History isn't just about the past - it's about how we use that knowledge to navigate our present and shape our future. Let's begin this journey through the most remarkable story ever told - the human story.

JANUARY

JANUARY 1

Early Hominids
The Origins of Humanity

4-2 million years ago

While we often picture early hominids as primitive cave dwellers, they were remarkable innovators who thrived across diverse African landscapes for millions of years. The discovery of "Lucy," a 3.2-million-year-old Australopithecus, revealed that our ancestors walked upright long before developing large brains, suggesting that bipedalism was the first major step in human evolution.

What's even more surprising is that early hominids weren't alone – they shared their world with several other human species. At times, up to six different human species coexisted on Earth, each adapting to different environments. Some were tall and built for running, while others were short and perfect for forest life.

Perhaps most remarkably, these early hominids survived as a minority species among much larger and more powerful animals. They weren't the strongest or fastest creatures, but their ability to adapt and work together allowed them to thrive in environments where individual survival would have been impossible. This early social cooperation laid the groundwork for human civilization.

Which evolutionary advantage developed first in early hominids?
A) Tool use and manipulation
B) Upright walking
C) Large brain size
D) Complex language

Answer: B

JANUARY 2

First Tools

The Origins of Humanity

3.3 million - 2 million years ago

The story of early human tools isn't just about rocks and bones – it's a tale of remarkable innovation that began far earlier than we once thought. The oldest known stone tools, discovered at Lomekwi, Kenya, date back to 3.3 million years ago, predating the earliest known Homo species by hundreds of thousands of years. This revolutionary discovery suggests that our pre-human ancestors were far more sophisticated than previously believed.

These ancient toolmakers didn't simply break rocks randomly – they developed specific techniques that required planning and forethought. By striking rocks at precise angles, they created sharp edges perfect for cutting meat and cracking bones for marrow. This complexity of thought and action occurred long before the evolution of larger brains, challenging our understanding of cognitive development.

Most surprisingly, these early tools weren't just used for hunting or butchering. Microscopic analysis of tool edges reveals they were also used for gathering and processing plants, suggesting our ancestors weren't the predominantly meat-eating hunters we once imagined. These tools helped access a diverse diet that ultimately fueled brain growth and human evolution.

What material were the earliest stone tools primarily made from?
A) Obsidian
B) Quartz
C) Basalt
D) Volcanic tuff

Answer: C

JANUARY 3

Fire Control
The Origins of Humanity

1 million - 400,000 years ago

The mastery of fire marks one of humanity's most profound achievements, but its origin story is more complex than simply learning to make flames. The earliest evidence of controlled fire use, found in Wonderwerk Cave in South Africa, dates back to one million years ago. However, these early humans didn't create fire – they maintained it, carrying embers from natural fires and keeping them alive for weeks or months.

The relationship between humans and fire transformed our species in unexpected ways. While we often focus on cooking's role in improving food safety and nutrition, fire's greatest impact may have been social. Gathering around evening fires extended day length, creating the first social spaces where stories could be shared and complex social bonds could form.

Most surprisingly, fire might have helped make us more resilient sleepers. As nighttime predator attacks became less frequent, humans could enter deeper sleep phases, potentially improving memory consolidation and cognitive development. This may have contributed to our species' rapid brain development and social learning capabilities.

Which development did fire control directly enable?
A) Tool making
B) Language development
C) Smaller teeth
D) Cave painting

Answer: C

7

JANUARY 4

Cave Art

The Origins of Humanity

40,000 - 15,000 years ago

The discovery of prehistoric cave art revolutionized our understanding of early human cognition and creativity. The most famous site, Lascaux Cave in France, contains over 2,000 figures painted roughly 17,000 years ago. But the oldest known cave art, found in Indonesia, dates back 45,500 years, suggesting that humans developed sophisticated artistic expression long before reaching Europe.

What's particularly fascinating is that these ancient artists developed complex techniques that rival modern methods. They created paints by mixing ochre, hematite, and charcoal with animal fat and water, and even developed primitive spray-painting techniques by blowing pigments through hollow bones. The artists also used the natural contours of cave walls to give their animals a three-dimensional appearance.

Scientific analysis of cave paintings has revealed an extraordinary fact: 75% of hand prints found in European cave art belonged to women, challenging long-held assumptions about gender roles in prehistoric societies. The findings suggest that women played a crucial role in developing early artistic traditions.

What percentage of animals depicted in European cave art were actually hunted for food, based on archaeological evidence?
A) 82%
B) 64%
C) 45%
D) 23%

Answer: D

Early Languages

The Origins of Humanity

100,000 - 50,000 years ago

While we often assume language emerged gradually over millions of years, many linguists now believe that complex language appeared relatively suddenly around 70,000 years ago, coinciding with an explosion of cultural innovations. This hypothesis is supported by genetic studies showing that mutations in FOXP2, a gene crucial for language development, became fixed in human populations during this period.

The emergence of complex language revolutionized human society. Unlike animal communication, human language enabled displaced reference—discussing absent things, including abstract concepts, past events, and future plans. This cognitive leap facilitated complex coordination and knowledge transmission across generations.

Modern analysis of existing languages has revealed that all human languages share approximately 300 core concepts that may date back to this original proto-language period. These universal concepts include basic words like "mother," "hand," and "fire," providing a linguistic window into our shared cognitive past.

What percentage of the estimated 300 universal words found across all human languages relate to survival-based concepts (tools, food, body parts)?
A) 47%
B) 63%
C) 75%
D) 89%

Answer: C

9

JANUARY 6

Early Spirituality

The Origins of Humanity

100,000 - 40,000 years ago

The origins of human spirituality extend far deeper into our past than previously imagined. Archaeological evidence suggests that Neanderthals were burying their dead with grave goods as early as 100,000 years ago, indicating they may have believed in an afterlife. These findings challenge our assumptions about the cognitive capabilities of our evolutionary cousins and the uniqueness of human spiritual thinking.

Spiritual beliefs may have served crucial evolutionary functions beyond comfort with death. Shared religious practices united large groups, enabling humans to form communities far larger than primatologists consider natural. This social cohesion through shared beliefs formed the foundation of human civilization.

Analysis of ancient burial sites has revealed that 84% of early human graves contained objects that had no practical use, suggesting deliberate ritual placement. These items often included red ochre, a mineral that had no practical value but appears in burial contexts across five continents, hinting at shared symbolic thinking among early humans.

What percentage of Neanderthal burial sites show evidence of intentional flower placement, based on pollen analysis?
A) 28%
B) 13%
C) 35%
D) 47%

Answer: A

JANUARY 7

The First Farmers
The Agricultural Revolution

12,000 - 10,000 BCE

The transition to farming wasn't the straightforward progress narrative we often imagine. Recent evidence suggests that early humans in the Fertile Crescent experimented with plant cultivation for thousands of years before fully embracing agriculture. These semi-sedentary communities maintained a complex hybrid lifestyle, combining wild food gathering with small-scale farming, challenging our notion of a clean break between hunter-gatherer and agricultural societies.

Early Middle Eastern farmers surprisingly cultivated multiple wheat and barley varieties simultaneously, creating backup systems against crop failure. They also formed complex social networks with hunter-gatherers, serving as early trade systems and food security.

Analysis of early agricultural sites reveals that pioneering farmers maintained an average of 7-9 different crop varieties, with some communities cultivating up to 12 distinct strains of wheat alone. This agricultural diversity exceeded that of many modern industrial farms.

Which innovative farming technique, still used by indigenous peoples today, did early agriculturalists develop to prevent soil exhaustion?
A) Crop rotation with legumes
B) Mixed elevation planting
C) Companion planting of cereals
D) Alternating field flooding

Answer: B

JANUARY 8

Early Villages

The Agricultural Revolution

9,000 - 7,000 BCE

The world's first villages weren't just smaller versions of later cities—they were radical experiments in human coexistence. Çatalhöyük, in modern-day Turkey, housed up to 10,000 people around 7000 BCE in a peculiar arrangement where houses were packed so tightly together that residents had to enter through the roof. There were no streets, suggesting a social organization fundamentally different from anything we know today.

These early settlements developed surprising solutions to urban living. Archaeological evidence from Çatalhöyük shows that residents regularly plastered and repainted their walls, not just for decoration but as a practical measure against disease-carrying pests. They also developed sophisticated waste management systems and practiced some of the earliest known forms of recycling.

The architectural density of Çatalhöyük was extraordinary: its 2,000 clustered buildings achieved a population density of 45,000 people per square kilometer in its core area—comparable to modern Manhattan's densest blocks.

What unexpected feature did archaeologists discover about Çatalhöyük's buildings?
A) Load-bearing walls contained human bones for reinforcement
B) Interior temperatures remained constant year-round
C) Houses were deliberately burned and rebuilt every 70-80 years
D) Wall plaster contained antibacterial copper compounds

Answer: C

JANUARY 9

Social Hierarchies
The Agricultural Revolution

7,000 - 5,000 BCE

The emergence of social hierarchy represents one of humanity's most profound transformations, yet it didn't develop as simply as we once thought. Recent archaeological evidence suggests that early agricultural communities maintained egalitarian structures for thousands of years before social stratification emerged. The catalyst wasn't farming itself, but the development of food storage and surplus management systems.

The first hierarchies weren't based on wealth or military power, but on the ability to organize communal labor and storage. Early leaders were often responsible for maintaining granaries and coordinating planting schedules. These "managers" gradually accumulated influence not through force, but through their role in ensuring community survival through lean times.

DNA analysis of remains from early agricultural settlements reveals that leadership positions in some communities were inherited through maternal lines for over 800 years before patrilineal systems became dominant.

What unique archaeological marker first indicated the emergence of social hierarchy?
A) Differential access to obsidian tools
B) Standardized grain measure vessels
C) Distinct house paint pigments
D) Specialized storage jar seals

Answer: D

JANUARY 10
Pottery and Tools
The Agricultural Revolution

8,000 - 6,000 BCE

The invention of pottery transformed human society in ways that went far beyond simple storage containers. While we often focus on pottery's role in storing grain, the earliest pottery was actually used for cooking, appearing first in East Asia around 20,000 years ago among hunter-gatherers. This discovery has forced archaeologists to rethink the traditional narrative about pottery's relationship to farming.

The development of ceramic technology led to unexpected innovations in other fields. The high-temperature firing techniques developed for pottery eventually enabled metalworking, while the need for specific clay types spurred the first mining operations. Early potters also developed sophisticated knowledge of chemistry, learning to control oxidation and reduction in their kilns centuries before formal scientific understanding.

Ancient pottery kilns achieved temperatures of up to 1000°C—hot enough to create chemical reactions that wouldn't be scientifically understood for another 7,000 years.

How many distinct hand positions have archaeologists identified in ancient fingerprints preserved on pottery, suggesting standardized manufacturing techniques?

A) 3
B) 7
C) 12
D) 15

Answer: C

JANUARY 11

Sumer and the First Cities

Mesopotamia and Early Civilizations

4,500 - 4,000 BCE

The rise of Sumerian cities marked humanity's first experiment with large-scale urban living, but these earliest cities defied our expectations. Uruk, the world's first true city, wasn't built around a palace or temple as once thought, but around a complex network of canals and reservoirs. This hydraulic system predated the city's famous ziggurats by several centuries, suggesting that environmental engineering, not religion, was the primary driver of early urbanization.

These early cities solved modern problems. Uruk's inhabitants built the world's first public sanitation system with elaborate drainage and waste management. They also created building codes to prevent structural failures in their tall buildings.

The scale of early Sumerian urban planning was staggering. Archaeological evidence shows that Uruk's canal system moved over 400,000 cubic meters of water daily—equivalent to 160 Olympic swimming pools—making it more efficient per capita than many modern cities' water systems.

What remarkable engineering feat did Uruk's early water management system achieve?
A) Operating without mechanical pumps for 23 generations
B) Supporting 6 harvests per year in surrounding fields
C) Maintaining water pressure equivalent to a modern 4-story building
D) Recycling 72% of its water through natural filtration

Answer: A

JANUARY 12

Invention of Writing

Mesopotamia and Early Civilizations

3,200 - 3,000 BCE

The invention of writing in ancient Sumer wasn't the sudden breakthrough we often imagine. Recent archaeological discoveries reveal a complex evolution spanning centuries, beginning with simple counting tokens used in trade. These tokens gradually evolved into impressed clay symbols, then pictographs, and finally the wedge-shaped marks we know as cuneiform.

What's particularly fascinating is that writing wasn't invented to record stories or laws, but to track economic transactions. The earliest texts are almost exclusively administrative records—lists of goods, payments, and debts. Literature and historical records came later, suggesting that the practical needs of commerce, not the desires of rulers or priests, drove this revolutionary innovation.

Early Sumerian scribes developed a standardized curriculum that required mastering exactly 1,000 cuneiform signs before qualification, though only about 600 were commonly used in daily writing.

Which mathematical concept was first recorded in cuneiform that wouldn't be reinvented for another 3,000 years?
A) The quadratic formula
B) The Pythagorean theorem
C) Zero as a placeholder
D) Negative numbers

Answer: C

16

JANUARY 13
Ziggurats and Temples
Mesopotamia and Early Civilizations

2,900 - 2,350 BCE

The massive ziggurats of ancient Mesopotamia weren't just temples—they were complex machines for urban organization. Recent archaeological work reveals that these structures served as administrative centers, grain banks, and astronomical observatories in addition to their religious functions. The famous Ziggurat of Ur contained not only shrines but also storage facilities, offices, and workshops.

These ancient skyscrapers employed sophisticated engineering techniques that wouldn't be rediscovered for millennia. Their builders used bitumen as waterproofing, created ventilation systems to prevent grain spoilage, and developed mathematical principles of structural load-bearing that wouldn't be formally understood until the modern era. They even incorporated seismic protection features in regions prone to earthquakes.

The construction of the Great Ziggurat of Ur required moving more than 8 million bricks, each weighing about 15 kg, yet analysis shows the structure's base deviates from perfectly level by less than 2 centimeters across its entire area.

What architectural feature of Mesopotamian ziggurats was accidentally rediscovered during the design of modern skyscrapers?
A) Harmonic vibration dampening
B) Self-cleaning external surfaces
C) Temperature-regulated air flow
D) Weight-distributing foundations

Answer: A

17

JANUARY 14

Hammurabi's Code

Mesopotamia and Early Civilizations

1,750 BCE

While Hammurabi's Code is famous as the first written legal system, its true innovation wasn't in creating new laws but in standardizing existing ones. The Code compiled and harmonized various local legal traditions, creating a uniform system across a diverse empire. Many of its laws were already in practice for centuries before being carved into stone.

What's particularly remarkable about the Code is its sophisticated understanding of economic incentives. Rather than simply punishing wrongdoing, many laws were designed to prevent disputes from arising in the first place. For example, builders were made personally liable for deaths caused by building collapses, effectively creating the world's first building safety regulations.

Analysis of the Code reveals that 57% of its laws dealt with economic matters, while only 13% addressed what we would today consider criminal behavior. This suggests an advanced understanding of law as a tool for commercial regulation rather than just punishment.

What unusual requirement in Hammurabi's Code created the world's first consumer protection law?
A) Mandatory product warranties
B) Public price listings
C) Quality control inspections
D) Standardized measurements

Answer: A

JANUARY 15

The Assyrian Empire
Mesopotamia and Early Civilizations

911 - 612 BCE

The Assyrian Empire wasn't just a military superpower—it was history's first systematic attempt at creating a multicultural state. While famous for their military prowess, the Assyrians developed sophisticated administrative systems that allowed diverse peoples to maintain their local customs while participating in a broader imperial culture.

Contrary to their reputation for brutality, the Assyrians were also great preservers of knowledge. King Ashurbanipal's library at Nineveh contained over 30,000 clay tablets, including multiple copies of important texts to ensure their preservation. This library represents history's first systematic attempt at collecting and preserving human knowledge.

Archaeological evidence suggests the Assyrian postal system could deliver messages across their entire empire—about 1,500 miles—in just five days, a speed that wouldn't be matched until the American Pony Express more than two millennia later.

Which innovative military technology, first developed by the Assyrians, wouldn't be improved upon until the 19th century?
A) Cavalry stirrups
B) Siege towers
C) Iron sword-making
D) Pontoon bridges

Answer: D

JANUARY 16
Mesopotamian Trade Networks
Mesopotamia and Early Civilizations

3,000 - 1,750 BCE

The ancient trade networks of Mesopotamia weren't just economic systems—they were the world's first information superhighways. Merchants didn't just exchange goods; they carried news, technologies, and ideas across vast distances. Recent evidence suggests that mathematical concepts like the 60-minute hour spread along these trade routes long before formal mathematical texts.

These networks were surprisingly sophisticated in their organization. Merchants developed complex financial instruments, including promissory notes and partnership agreements, thousands of years before the invention of modern banking. They even created the first international trade agreements, complete with standardized weights and measures.

Chemical analysis of artifacts has revealed that a single merchant caravan around 2000 BCE might carry goods sourced from up to 14 different regions, spanning distances of over 2,000 miles from source to destination.

Which Mesopotamian banking innovation wouldn't be reinvented until Renaissance Italy?
A) Commodity futures
B) Letters of credit
C) Insurance contracts
D) Joint-stock companies

Answer: A

JANUARY 17

The Babylonian Captivity
Mesopotamia and Early Civilizations

597 - 539 BCE

The Babylonian Captivity wasn't the straightforward mass deportation often depicted in historical accounts. Archaeological evidence shows that only about 25% of Judah's population—primarily the elite and skilled craftsmen—were actually taken to Babylon. This selective deportation was part of a sophisticated Babylonian strategy to neutralize potential resistance while acquiring valuable human capital.

The exiled Jews in Babylon enjoyed surprising freedoms. Cuneiform tablets from the period show that many Jews became successful merchants and royal contractors, with some even serving as tax collectors and administrators. They were allowed to live in their own communities, maintain their customs, and even operate their own internal justice system.

The captivity period transformed Judaism in unexpected ways. The need to maintain religious identity without a temple led to the development of synagogues and the compilation of written religious texts. Analysis of religious documents shows that approximately 70% of modern Jewish liturgical practices originated during this period of exile.

What percentage of Jewish families in Babylon, according to cuneiform records, owned their own businesses by 570 BCE?
A) 23%
B) 37%
C) 52%
D) 64%

Answer: C

21

JANUARY 18

African Kingdoms
African Cultural Development

800 BCE - 300 CE

The kingdom of Kush, often overshadowed by its northern neighbor Egypt, was a technological powerhouse that revolutionized iron production. Their distinctive furnaces, which used a bellows system with multiple tuyères (specialized ceramic pipes for directing airflow), achieved temperatures of 1,250°C—hundreds of degrees hotter than contemporary furnaces in Europe and Asia.

Kushite pyramids, beyond royal tombs, served as sophisticated astronomical calendars. Their alignment accurately predicted the annual Nile flooding within two days, aiding Kush's development of a highly productive agricultural system.

Recent satellite archaeology has revealed that the Kushite capital of Meroe was surrounded by an industrial zone covering over 6 square kilometers—comparable in size to the industrial districts of ancient Rome. Analysis of slag deposits suggests that Meroe's furnaces produced approximately 25,000 tons of iron annually during their peak production period.

How many tuyères (air pipes) did the typical Kushite furnace use to achieve its superior temperatures? (For context, most ancient furnaces used 1-2)
A) 4-6 tuyères
B) 8-12 tuyères
C) 14-18 tuyères
D) 20-24 tuyères

Answer: B

22

JANUARY 19
The Empire of Ghana
African Cultural Development

300 - 1200 CE

The Empire of Ghana (not related to modern Ghana) revolutionized trans-Saharan trade through its sophisticated customs system. Archaeological evidence shows that the empire maintained a network of 47 official trading posts across the Sahara, spaced precisely one camel-day's journey apart—roughly 25 miles. This standardization created history's first regulated trade corridor across a major desert.

Ghana's capital, Koumbi Saleh, was actually two cities in one—a unique urban planning concept that wouldn't be seen again until modern diplomatic capitals. The royal city housed the administration and traditional religious practitioners, while the Muslim merchant city (located 6 kilometers away) handled international trade. This dual-city system allowed for religious tolerance while maintaining traditional governance.

Examination of surviving merchant records shows that Ghana's trade volume was staggering: during peak periods, camel caravans transported approximately 12 metric tons of gold northward annually—equivalent to about 2% of today's global gold production.

What percentage of the world's imported gold passed through Ghana's trading network at its peak in 1000 CE?
A) 47%
B) 63%
C) 79%
D) 85%

Answer: C

23

The Swahili City-States
African Cultural Development

900 - 1500 CE

The Swahili coast wasn't just a trading region—it was medieval globalization in action. Archaeological analysis of a single merchant house in Kilwa has revealed artifacts from 43 different regions, spanning from China to Spain. The Swahili traders developed a sophisticated commodity exchange system, where goods might change hands up to 12 times before reaching their final destination.

These coastal cities developed advanced architectural techniques that combined local materials with global engineering knowledge. Their distinctive coral-rag architecture (buildings made from coral reef limestone) used a complex mortar system that actually grew stronger with exposure to seawater—a feature that modern marine engineers are only now beginning to replicate.

Chemical analysis of Swahili pottery reveals that their craftsmen developed unique glazing techniques that required kilns to maintain precise temperatures (within a 5-degree Celsius range) for over 30 hours—a level of control that European potters wouldn't achieve until the 18th century.

What percentage of Swahili buildings from 1200-1500 CE used the self-strengthening coral-rag technique? (The technique required extensive knowledge of both architecture and marine chemistry)
A) 31%
B) 45%
C) 67%
D) 82%

Answer: B

24

JANUARY 21

Great Zimbabwe
African Cultural Development

1100 - 1450 CE

Great Zimbabwe wasn't just a city—it was an architectural marvel that required unprecedented organizational skills. The Great Enclosure's outer wall contains approximately 900,000 stone blocks, each weighing between 20 and 50 kilograms, all fitted without mortar. Statistical analysis shows that completing this construction required moving an average of 1,000 blocks per day over a three-year period.

The city's builders, skilled in acoustics and crowd management, designed the conical tower and parallel passages of the Great Enclosure to amplify a speaker's voice and dampen ambient noise— a feat that modern acoustic science would only later fully comprehend.

Recent archaeological studies using ground-penetrating radar have revealed that Great Zimbabwe's water management system included over 15 kilometers of underground channels that could store approximately 2 million liters of water—enough to support a population of 20,000 through a 90-day dry season.

What unique mathematical ratio, later rediscovered in Renaissance architecture, did Great Zimbabwe's builders use in their wall construction?
A) The golden ratio (1:1.618)
B) The builders' triangle (3:4:5)
C) The acoustic seventh (4:7)
D) The Zimbabwe ratio (5:8:13)

Answer: A

25

JANUARY 22

Timbuktu: A Center of Learning

African Cultural Development

1200 - 1600 CE

Timbuktu's intellectual achievement wasn't just its famous libraries—it was the scale of its educational system. At its peak, the city maintained 150-180 Quranic schools alongside three major universities, with the largest, Sankore, enrolling over 25,000 students. Contemporary records show that approximately 1 in 4 of Timbuktu's residents was either a student or scholar.

Timbuktu's scriptoria produced books at an astonishing rate. Analysis of paper imports shows scribes used 70 metric tons annually, more than contemporary London or Paris. Each master scribe trained 12 apprentices, creating a sophisticated system for knowledge preservation.

Sankore University's curriculum was diverse, requiring students to master 70 subjects, from astronomy to jurisprudence, with specialized tracks needing up to 17 years of study. Surviving manuscripts show that 40% of texts covered subjects other than religion, like mathematics, medicine, and astronomy.

What percentage of Timbuktu's manuscripts included original marginal annotations, suggesting active scholarly debate rather than mere copying? (This rate exceeds that of medieval European universities)
A) 37%
B) 52%
C) 68%
D) 83%

Answer: C

JANUARY 23

The Rise of Egypt

Ancient Egypt: Power of the Nile

3100 - 2686 BCE

The unification of Egypt wasn't just a political achievement—it was history's first large-scale exercise in standardization. Archaeological evidence shows that within just three generations, the unified kingdom had standardized everything from pottery dimensions to architectural cubits (a unit of measurement). Analysis of artifacts reveals that measurement variations decreased from 30% to less than 1% across a distance of 800 kilometers.

Early Egyptian administration developed sophisticated methods for managing large-scale projects. The Step Pyramid complex at Saqqara required coordinating 8,000 workers over 19 years. Administrators used a complex system of tokens and seals to track materials and labor with an accuracy rate of 98.5%.

The development of hieroglyphic writing transformed record-keeping. Statistical analysis of early administrative texts shows that scribes could track up to 200 different commodities simultaneously, with error rates below 0.5%—a level of accuracy that wouldn't be matched until the invention of double-entry bookkeeping in Renaissance Italy.

What unexpected innovation enabled Egyptian administrators to achieve such remarkable accuracy in their record-keeping?
A) Multiple independent audits
B) Decimal-based counting
C) Color-coded clay tokens
D) Base-10 mathematical notation combined with pictographs

Answer: D

27

JANUARY 24

The Pyramids

Ancient Egypt: Power of the Nile

2686 - 2181 BCE

The construction of the Great Pyramid wasn't just an engineering marvel—it was a logistical one as well. Recent research shows that the core workforce was around 20,000 skilled craftsmen (not slaves), with support staff bringing the total to 30,000, all organized into teams of 200, each specializing in specific tasks.

The precision of the pyramid still amazes modern engineers. The base deviates from a perfect square by just 7.9 millimeters, and its corners align with the cardinal directions with an error of less than 0.15 degrees. These feats required advanced surveying techniques, not improved upon until the invention of laser theodolites.

The internal temperature of the pyramid remains constant at 20°C, thanks to its air shafts, limestone insulation, and precise geometry—a level of stability that modern buildings typically achieve only with active HVAC systems.

What percentage of the stones were cut so precisely that the gaps between them are less than 0.5 millimeters? (For context, modern building standards typically allow gaps of 2-3 millimeters)
A) 53%
B) 67%
C) 78%
D) 85%

Answer: C

JANUARY 25
Egyptian Religion
Ancient Egypt: Power of the Nile

3100 - 30 BCE

Egyptian religion wasn't just a belief system—it was one of history's first attempts at creating a unified theory of existence. Analysis of religious texts shows that Egyptian priests developed a complex cosmology that integrated mathematics, astronomy, and natural philosophy. Their religious calendar predicted solar and lunar events with an accuracy of 99.7% over a 500-year cycle.

Temples in ancient Egypt served as economic centers, with Karnak controlling agricultural lands equivalent to 15% of Egypt's arable territory. Temple records show sophisticated resource management systems, including crop rotation and water conservation techniques.

Modern analysis reveals Egyptian priests used advanced acoustic engineering in ceremonial spaces. Karnak's grand hall amplifies certain frequencies while dampening others, creating specific acoustic effects for religious ceremonies. Stones were cut and positioned to achieve resonant frequencies matching vowel sounds in ancient Egyptian chanting.

What percentage of Egyptian temple revenue was reinvested in public works and grain storage, essentially creating the world's first social welfare system?
A) 23%
B) 34%
C) 42%
D) 57%

Answer: C

JANUARY 26

The Middle Kingdom

Ancient Egypt: Power of the Nile

2055 - 1650 BCE

The Middle Kingdom revolutionized ancient bureaucracy with sophisticated administrative systems. Scribal records show government officials tracked over 3 million individual tax assessments annually with error rates below 0.7%, a level of accuracy normally only achieved through computerization. This was achieved through a hierarchical system of checks and balances involving at least three officials.

Middle Kingdom engineering projects showcased unprecedented water management precision. The Fayum irrigation system, centered around Lake Moeris, used dams and channels to maintain depth variations of less than 2 centimeters across a 100-square-kilometer area. This system doubled Egypt's agricultural productivity in the region.

The world's first systematic civil service examinations emerged during this period. Scribal candidates needed 85% accuracy in calculations and writing to qualify. This meritocratic system allowed about 28% of high-ranking officials to come from non-elite backgrounds.

What percentage of Middle Kingdom administrative documents show evidence of the triple-verification system (recognizable by three distinct handwritings per entry)?

A) 73%
B) 81%
C) 89%
D) 94%

Answer: D

JANUARY 27

Akhenaten's Reforms

Ancient Egypt: Power of the Nile

1353 - 1336 BCE

Akhenaten's religious revolution, not only theological but also historical, aimed to completely restructure society's belief system. Within a decade, his administration modified 85,000 inscriptions across Egypt, replacing traditional imagery with new iconography. This involved mobilizing 4,000 skilled artisans and developing standardized artistic techniques.

The construction of his new capital, Akhetaten (modern Tell el-Amarna), represented an unprecedented urban planning experiment. Built in just 15 years, the city incorporated exact astronomical alignments—modern satellite analysis shows that major boulevards were oriented to create specific shadow patterns during solar events, with precision to within 0.3 degrees.

Archaeological analysis of Amarna's residential areas has revealed the world's first known urban zoning system. The city was divided into ten districts, each with specific building codes that regulated everything from wall thickness to window placement. Housing density varied systematically, from 65 persons per hectare in elite areas to 200 persons per hectare in artisan quarters.

What fraction of Amarna's buildings incorporated the standardized "solar window" feature (clerestory windows designed to track the sun's path)?
A) One-third
B) Two-fifths
C) Three-quarters
D) Four-fifths

Answer: C

31

JANUARY 28

Tutankhamun's Legacy

Ancient Egypt: Power of the Nile

1332 - 1323 BCE

Tutankhamun's tomb wasn't just a treasury—it was a time capsule that revolutionized our understanding of ancient Egyptian material culture. The tomb contained 5,398 cataloged items, including 2,000 pieces of clothing and 139 walking sticks. Statistical analysis of the artifacts reveals that 84% of them were created specifically for the afterlife, suggesting an enormous mobilization of craftsmen during the 70-day mummification period.

The preservation techniques used in the tomb demonstrated remarkable sophistication. Environmental monitoring has shown that the tomb's design maintained a constant relative humidity of 42% (±3%) for over 3,000 years without any active systems. This perfect preservation environment was created through careful material selection and architectural design.

Tutankhamun's gold mask, constructed using unique techniques, remained unrivaled until the 20th century. It combines two gold alloys, creating a bi-metallic effect that prevented warping for millennia. The gold's thickness varies by less than 0.2mm across its surface—a level of precision that modern metalworkers struggle to achieve.

What percentage of organic materials in Tutankhamun's tomb survived intact due to the precise environmental conditions?
A) 58%
B) 67%
C) 73%
D) 82%

Answer: C

32

JANUARY 29

The Fall of Ancient Egypt

Ancient Egypt: Power of the Nile

343 - 30 BCE

The decline of ancient Egypt wasn't the sudden collapse often portrayed—it was a complex process that transformed the world's longest-lasting civilization. Climate data derived from Nile flood records shows that rainfall patterns began shifting around 1000 BCE, with flood reliability dropping from 92% to 67% over three centuries. This environmental change forced fundamental alterations in Egypt's administrative and agricultural systems.

Egypt's final centuries saw remarkable technological innovations. Late Period irrigation systems developed water-lifting devices that raised water up to 8 meters, increasing efficiency by 45% compared to traditional methods.

In administration, Egypt pioneered the world's first known pension system for state workers. Retired scribes received 66% of their working income, while disabled workers could get up to 83%. This system remained the most comprehensive until 19th century Prussia.

What percentage of Egyptian agricultural land remained independently managed by temples in 30 BCE, despite multiple foreign conquests?
A) 12%
B) 23%
C) 31%
D) 42%

Answer: C

33

The Harappan Civilization
The Indus Valley and Early China

3300 - 1300 BCE

The Indus Valley civilization wasn't just another ancient society—it was history's first urban culture to achieve precise standardization across multiple cities. Archaeological evidence shows that 96% of Harappan bricks conform to a ratio of 4:2:1, regardless of their size or location. This standardization extended across sites separated by more than 1,500 kilometers.

Harappan water management systems were highly sophisticated. The Great Bath of Mohenjo-daro used a complex filtration system that processed 23,000 liters of water per hour through gravel and charcoal. It maintained water purity levels similar to modern secondary treatment facilities.

Recent satellite analysis has revealed that Harappan cities were oriented according to astronomical alignments with an accuracy of 0.1 degrees. Furthermore, the distance between major urban centers appears to follow a precise mathematical progression based on units of 8.4 kilometers—suggesting the existence of a sophisticated urban planning system spanning the entire civilization.

What fraction of Harappan residential structures incorporated a private bathing area with direct access to the municipal drainage system? (A level of sanitation that wouldn't be matched until 19th century London)
A) 1/6
B) 1/3
C) 1/2
D) 2/3

Answer: B

JANUARY 31
Trade in the Indus Valley
The Indus Valley and Early China

2600 - 1900 BCE

The Indus Valley trading network wasn't just extensive—it was history's first example of standardized commercial integration across a subcontinental scale. Archaeological evidence shows that weights and measures found at sites spanning 800,000 square kilometers varied by less than 0.1%, indicating remarkable standardization over a vast area.

Harappan merchants developed sophisticated quality control systems. Analysis of shell bangles (a major trade item) shows that 94% met standardized specifications for thickness and diameter, with variations of less than 0.5mm. This level of precision required developing complex manufacturing processes and training systems that were transmitted across multiple production centers.

The scale of Harappan trade was staggering. A single warehouse discovered at Lothal could store approximately 465,000 liters of grain, with advanced ventilation systems that prevented spoilage for up to three years. Computer modeling suggests that the total storage capacity of major Harappan cities could sustain the entire civilization for 2.7 years without additional production.

What percentage of Harappan seals (used for marking trade goods) show evidence of a standardized quality control system involving multiple inspections?
A) 77%
B) 83%
C) 89%
D) 95%

Answer: C

FEBRUARY

FEBRUARY 1

The Shang Dynasty

The Indus Valley and Early China

1600 - 1046 BCE

Shang Dynasty metalworkers revolutionized ancient metallurgy through unprecedented standardization. Their bronze vessels maintained precise alloy ratios: 83% copper, 15% tin, and 2% lead, with variations of less than 0.5%. This consistency required sophisticated supply chain management across hundreds of kilometers.

The Shang capital at Anyang pioneered astronomical urban planning. Recent archaeological surveys reveal the city's precise alignment with celestial movements, allowing major buildings to cast specific shadows during solstices and equinoxes. The central palace complex tracked seasonal changes with an accuracy of ±0.3 days through architectural alignments alone.

Oracle bone archives demonstrate remarkable administrative sophistication. Scribes tracked resources, population movements, and harvests across 1.2 million square kilometers using a standardized writing system of over 4,000 distinct characters.

What unexpected ingredient did Shang Dynasty rulers add to their ceremonial wines?

A) Crushed meteorites (believed to capture celestial power)
B) Powdered jade (thought to grant immortality)
C) Ground tiger bones (meant to transfer strength)
D) Liquid mercury (intended to extend life)

Answer: A

FEBRUARY 2

Oracle Bones and Divination

The Indus Valley and Early China

1250 - 1046 BCE

The systematic data collection of Shang Dynasty oracle bones marked history's first empirical record-keeping system. Among 157,000 known oracle bone fragments, approximately 68% contain verifiable astronomical or meteorological observations, creating an unprecedented scientific archive.

Production of oracle bones required sophisticated quality control systems. Craftsmen sourced cattle scapulae and turtle plastrons from regions up to 1,000 kilometers away, processing them through a standardized 12-step preparation procedure. Chemical analysis reveals precise preparation techniques suggesting centralized production facilities.

Advanced technological precision defined oracle bone inscriptions. Electron microscopy shows specialized tools achieved line widths of 0.1 millimeters—matching modern technical drafting precision. The character strokes exhibit standardized angles and proportions, revealing a sophisticated writing education system.

How many oracle bone fragments have archaeologists found with ancient Chinese "knock knock" jokes carved into them?

A) None - they were purely religious
B) 3 - all about door-knocking spirits
C) 12 - mostly riddles about ancestors
D) 7 - including the world's oldest recorded pun

Answer: D

38

FEBRUARY 3

Chinese Bronze Age

The Indus Valley and Early China

1700 - 400 BCE

Chinese Bronze Age technology pioneered standardized industrial production. A single Shang foundry produced up to 200 bronze vessels monthly, maintaining remarkable consistency between pieces through sophisticated quality control and material management systems.

The scale of production transformed ancient metallurgy. Major production centers processed approximately 330 metric tons of copper and 40 tons of tin annually. This massive operation spawned complex mining networks extending across multiple provinces, with shaft mines reaching depths of 100 meters.

The technical mastery culminated in works like the Houmuwu ding, weighing 832.84 kg and cast in a single piece. The vessel's walls maintained precise engineering tolerances throughout, demonstrating unprecedented control over the casting process.

What surprising sound effect did ancient Chinese bronze bells achieve that modern metallurgists still can't replicate?

A) Two distinct notes from one strike
B) Echoes that increase in volume
C) Harmonics that change with temperature
D) Vibrations that last for over an hour

Answer: A

FEBRUARY 4

The Mandate of Heaven

The Indus Valley and Early China

1046 - 256 BCE

The Mandate of Heaven established revolutionary principles of political authority. Zhou dynasty texts reveal sophisticated criteria for evaluating rulers, including harvest yields, disaster response, and military success. This system transformed traditional concepts of royal power.

This political innovation created remarkable social mobility in government service. By 800 BCE, officials from diverse backgrounds served in high-ranking positions, establishing new patterns of administrative recruitment. Their examination system would influence government structures for three millennia.

The Zhou dynasty pioneered sophisticated record-keeping systems. Their detailed annual records of agricultural output, population changes, and natural disasters achieved remarkable accuracy when compared to archaeological and climatological evidence.

Which Zhou Dynasty emperor's odd behavior first inspired the concept of the Mandate of Heaven?

A) He filled his palace with cats to act as advisors
B) He built a lake of wine and forced courtiers to row across it
C) He shot arrows at his subjects to test their loyalty
D) He appointed his horse as prime minister

Answer: B

FEBRUARY 5
Chinese Silk Production
The Indus Valley and Early China

3000 BCE - 200 CE

Ancient Chinese sericulturists pioneered sophisticated biological engineering. Through selective breeding, they developed silkworms producing threads 86% stronger than their wild counterparts. Modern analysis reveals these domesticated silkworms underwent remarkable genetic modifications.

The sophistication of silk production established new quality control standards. Han dynasty records describe a multi-stage production process, with specific temperature and humidity requirements for each stage. Archaeological evidence shows major silk workshops maintained precise environmental controls through architectural design and ventilation systems.

Silk production created revolutionary manufacturing processes. Workshop records show specialized teams focusing on specific production stages, with materials moving through multiple skilled craftspeople before completion. This system transformed ancient manufacturing methods.

What unexpected use did Chinese military commanders find for silkworms during sieges?

A) Early biological warfare (catapulting them over walls)
B) Emergency food supply
C) Soundproofing armor with cocoons
D) Testing for poison in food

Answer: C

FEBRUARY 6

The Causes of The Collapse
The Bronze Age Collapse

1200 - 1150 BCE

The Bronze Age collapse marked history's first documented system-wide failure of interconnected societies. Within just 5o years, 47% of known settlements in the Eastern Mediterranean faced destruction or abandonment. Cities that had thrived for a millennium disappeared within a single generation.

Recent climate studies using deep-sea sediment cores reveal dramatic environmental changes. Rainfall decreased by 3o% over three decades, while temperature proxy data indicates a 2°C average temperature rise. These climate shifts devastated agricultural systems that had sustained complex societies for centuries.

The collapse occurred with unprecedented speed. Trading networks moving tons of copper and tin across thousands of kilometers ceased operating within 25 years. Literacy rates among administrative classes plummeted, indicating rapid societal dissolution.

What bizarre phenomenon did survivors of collapsed cities report seeing in the sky?

A) Three consecutive solar eclipses
B) A year without stars
C) Red snow falling for 4o days
D) The moon appearing green

Answer: C

FEBRUARY 7

The Sea Peoples

The Bronze Age Collapse

1220 - 1150 BCE

The Sea Peoples launched history's first documented mass migration by sea. Egyptian records describe fleets of up to 900 ships, each carrying approximately 50 people, coordinating movements of entire communities. These fleets transported not just warriors but families, craftsmen, and farmers.

Naval archaeological discoveries have revealed revolutionary ship design. The Sea Peoples developed hull designs reducing water resistance by 32% compared to contemporary vessels. Modern reconstructions show these ships maintained remarkable speed while carrying substantial cargo.

The migration transformed Mediterranean civilization. Within one generation, most major coastal cities in the Eastern Mediterranean underwent dramatic changes. Recent archaeological evidence indicates complex patterns of cultural exchange and adaptation in rebuilt settlements.

What unexpected cargo have archaeologists found on several sunken Sea Peoples' ships?

A) Live monkeys in ceramic cages
B) Board games with written rules
C) Musical instruments with notation
D) Seeds from extinct plants

Answer: B

43

The Fall of Mycenaean Greece
The Bronze Age Collapse

1200 - 1100 BCE

The collapse of Mycenaean civilization marked history's first documented loss of a complex writing system. The Linear B script, recording 87 years of detailed palace administration, vanished completely. Administrative literacy disappeared within two generations.

Archaeological surveys reveal systematic patterns of abandonment. Among 320 known settlements, most faced abandonment or destruction within 75 years. Destruction layers show selective targeting: palaces suffered extensive damage while many surrounding settlements remained intact.

The collapse triggered dramatic technological regression. Mycenaean pottery production and metallurgy declined sharply, reverting to simpler techniques and smaller scales of production. Complex manufacturing systems gave way to basic production methods.

Which Mycenaean palace feature continues to puzzle modern architects?

A) Perfect acoustics that amplify whispers to shouts
B) Corridors that naturally maintain 20°C year-round
C) Walls that glow faintly in moonlight
D) Floors that never accumulate dust

Answer: B

FEBRUARY 9

The End of the Hittites

The Bronze Age Collapse

1190 - 1160 BCE

The Hittite Empire pioneered sophisticated diplomatic systems before its collapse. Their network managed numerous vassal states through complex treaties, processing hundreds of international agreements annually in five different languages.

Archaeological evidence reveals intense militarization preceding the collapse. During the empire's final decades, major Hittite centers devoted enormous resources to defensive construction, creating an unsustainable economic burden.

Climate reconstruction through pollen analysis shows devastating environmental changes. The region experienced severe rainfall decrease over three decades, disrupting an agricultural system supporting millions of people. Grain storage records indicate steady decline in reserves during the empire's final years.

What surprising skill were all Hittite royal children required to master?

A) Taming wild horses
B) Walking on hot coals
C) Speaking five languages
D) Swimming in full armor

Answer: D

FEBRUARY 10

Egypt's Survival
The Bronze Age Collapse

1177 - 1130 BCE

Egyptian administrative resilience distinguished it during the Bronze Age collapse. The bureaucracy maintained remarkable functionality while neighboring civilizations crumbled. Despite significant drops in Nile flood levels, their grain distribution system preserved social stability.

Strategic military adaptation proved crucial to survival. Within one generation, Egypt redirected military resources from offensive chariot forces to defensive infantry and naval units. This tactical shift successfully repelled multiple invasions while maintaining internal order.

Administrative excellence enabled effective crisis management. The bureaucracy's detailed population registers across 42 nomes (provinces) facilitated efficient resource distribution. Records document successful relocation of vulnerable populations to stable areas within 20 years.

What unique method did Egyptian priests use to predict Nile flood levels?

A) Measuring spider web angles
B) Counting sacred cat sneezes
C) Observing ibis migration patterns
D) Testing crocodile egg shells

Answer: A

FEBRUARY 11

Cultural Aftermath in Mesopotamia

The Bronze Age Collapse

1200 - 1000 BCE

Mesopotamian society preserved crucial elements of literacy through severe disruption. Surviving cuneiform tablets show that isolated centers of literacy maintained essential cultural knowledge despite widespread institutional collapse.

Cities underwent dramatic transformation for survival. Surviving urban centers shrank dramatically but demonstrated remarkable adaptation. The proportion of urban land devoted to food production increased significantly, establishing new patterns of city organization.

Trade patterns evolved toward local resilience. While long-distance luxury trade declined sharply, local exchange networks intensified. Pottery distribution analysis reveals dramatic shifts toward local production and exchange, creating more sustainable economic patterns.

What unexpected innovation emerged from post-collapse Mesopotamian cities?

A) Underground air conditioning systems
B) Soundproof meditation chambers
C) Color-changing road markers
D) Self-filling water clocks

Answer: A

47

FEBRUARY 12
The Rise of Iron Technology
The Bronze Age Collapse

1200 - 1000 BCE

Iron technology revolutionized ancient metallurgy through new production patterns. Iron ore's widespread availability transformed metalworking from centralized to distributed production, marking a fundamental shift in manufacturing patterns.

Regional innovation drove rapid advancement in iron working. Analysis of early iron artifacts reveals diverse technical developments across different regions. Success rates in achieving consistent hardness varied significantly, demonstrating parallel innovation paths.

Early ironsmiths achieved remarkable technical sophistication through experimentation. By 1000 BCE, some workshops produced steel with precisely controlled carbon content, matching precision levels unreached for millennia.

What strange ritual did early iron smiths perform to ensure successful smelting?

A) Singing to the ore for 3 days
B) Only working during full moons
C) Wearing copper masks
D) Dancing backwards around the furnace

Answer: C

48

FEBRUARY 13

Mycenaean Civilization

Classical Greece: Philosophy and Politics

1600 - 1100 BCE

Mycenaean civilization established the Mediterranean's first complex bureaucratic society. Administrators tracked tens of thousands of transactions annually, managing everything from textile production to military supplies with remarkable precision.

The scale of Mycenaean engineering achieved unprecedented feats. The Treasury of Atreus employed massive stones weighing up to 120 tons, with a 40-ton keystone. Computer modeling indicates sophisticated mathematical knowledge for calculating leverage and stress points, creating a dome that has stood for 3,300 years without mortar.

Mycenaean industrial production pioneered standardization. Palace workshops produced hundreds of standardized bronze items annually, maintaining precise weight tolerances between pieces. This consistency required complex quality control systems and specialized worker training.

What surprising entertainment feature has been found in every excavated Mycenaean palace?

A) Water-powered puppet theaters
B) Musical stairs
C) Echo chambers for storytelling
D) Mechanical bird imitators

Answer: B

49

FEBRUARY 14

The Greek Dark Ages

Classical Greece: Philosophy and Politics

1100 - 800 BCE

The Greek Dark Ages fostered dramatic societal transformation. New forms of community organization emerged from the ashes of Mycenaean civilization, establishing social patterns that would shape Greek culture for centuries to come. These settlements pioneered new approaches to community governance and resource sharing.

Technological adaptation flourished amid cultural changes. Iron working technology spread rapidly, with iron artifacts increasing by 600% over 200 years. Tools showed increasingly sophisticated manufacturing techniques despite the loss of centralized administration.

The period saw profound changes in social gathering and ritual. Archaeological evidence reveals new types of communal spaces and meeting halls appearing across settlements, transforming how communities made decisions and maintained social bonds. These innovations laid the cultural foundation for later Greek political institutions.

What unexpected skill survived the Greek Dark Age when writing was lost?

A) Complex astronomy calculations
B) Multi-color textile dyeing
C) Glass lens crafting
D) Mechanical clock making

Answer: B

The Rise of City-States

Classical Greece: Philosophy and Politics

800 - 600 BCE

Greek city-states pioneered systematic political experimentation. Within two centuries, approximately 800 independent poleis emerged, each developing distinct approaches to governance and civic organization. These cities became laboratories for new forms of political and social organization.

The transformation of civic life reshaped urban landscapes. Cities devoted substantial resources to creating new types of public spaces and civic buildings. These architectural innovations reflected the changing relationship between citizens and their government, establishing patterns that would influence urban design for centuries.

Political participation transformed Greek society. Cities developed sophisticated systems for citizen involvement in governance, creating new institutions and procedures for public decision-making. These innovations established precedents for collective governance that would influence political thought throughout history.

What bizarre law did every Greek city-state share despite their differences?

A) Citizens must nap after lunch
B) No whistling at sunset
C) Required daily exercise
D) Public singing on birthdays

Answer: C

The Rise of Sparta

Classical Greece: Philosophy and Politics

800 - 500 BCE

Spartan military society pioneered systematic education and training. The agoge system began at age 7 and lasted 13 years, transforming young boys into elite warriors through rigorous physical and mental conditioning. This revolutionary program achieved unprecedented standardization in military training.

Archaeological evidence has revealed sophisticated Spartan logistics. Their army could mobilize with remarkable speed, supported by an innovative system of supply caches and standardized equipment. This organizational efficiency surpassed all contemporary military forces.

The Spartan phalanx achieved extraordinary battlefield cohesion. Training enabled units to maintain formation integrity through extended combat operations, coordinating complex maneuvers while preserving tight shield-wall formations. Their disciplined approach revolutionized ancient warfare.

What surprising food did young Spartans have to steal without getting caught?

A) Honey from wild bees
B) Cheese from temple stores
C) Figs from sacred trees
D) Fish from royal ponds

Answer: B

The Persian Wars

Classical Greece: Philosophy and Politics

499 - 449 BCE

The Persian Wars they represented history's first documented clash between centralized and decentralized political systems. Persian forces, drawing from 23 satrapies (provinces), fielded an army of approximately 180,000 troops against a Greek alliance of 31 city-states mustering about 42,000 soldiers. Yet the Greeks' decentralized command structure proved remarkably resilient.

Recent archaeological studies of the Battle of Marathon have revealed sophisticated tactical innovations. Greek commanders discovered that troops running 200 meters in full armor (about 30 kg) could maintain formation cohesion while building enough momentum to break enemy lines. Data from experimental archaeology shows this tactic generated impact forces approximately 60% greater than traditional walking attacks.

Analysis of Persian and Greek military records shows a fascinating logistical contrast. The Persian army required approximately 1,500 tons of supplies daily, delivered through a complex bureaucratic system. Greek forces, operating from independent city-states, could sustain operations with just 100-150 tons of locally-sourced supplies per day, demonstrating superior logistical efficiency.

What unlikely animal helped the Greeks win a crucial battle against the Persians?
A) Trained dolphins disrupting ship anchors
B) Battle pigs covered in oil and set aflame
C) Stampeding cattle with torches attached
D) Attack dogs painted to look like lions

Answer: B

53

FEBRUARY 18

The Golden Age of Athens

Classical Greece: Philosophy and Politics

480 - 404 BCE

Athenian democracy was history's first large-scale experiment in direct citizen governance. At its peak, the Athenian assembly (Ecclesia) involved approximately 30,000 citizens, with regular meetings attracting 6,000-8,000 participants. Computer modeling suggests their sophisticated voting system could process 25 separate decisions in a single six-hour session.

The Periclean building program transformed construction technology. The Parthenon's columns incorporate a slight bulge (entasis) that compensates for optical illusion—they curve outward by exactly 1.7 centimeters at one-third of their height. This precision required developing new architectural planning techniques that wouldn't be fully understood until the Renaissance.

Public funding for arts and culture reached unprecedented levels. Records show that Athens spent approximately 800 talents annually on cultural programs (equivalent to the cost of building 400 warships), with about 60% of citizens attending state-sponsored theatrical performances. This created history's first documented creative economy, employing thousands in cultural production.

What unconventional substance did Athenian actors use to amplify their voices in outdoor theaters?
A) Fermented honey
B) Copper mouth resonators
C) Snake venom dilutions
D) Ground crystal mixtures

Answer: B

Socratic Philosophy

Classical Greece: Philosophy and Politics

470 - 399 BCE

Socrates didn't just create a new philosophical method—he developed history's first documented system of structured critical thinking. Analysis of Plato's dialogues reveals that the Socratic method follows a precise pattern: each dialogue contains an average of 12.3 question sequences, with each sequence targeting a specific logical assumption using a three-tiered questioning structure.

The impact of Socratic teaching was quantifiable. Records show that his direct students established 27 different philosophical schools across the Mediterranean, with second-generation students founding another 84 institutions. Within three generations, an estimated 8,000 students had been trained in Socratic methodology.

Recent textual analysis using AI algorithms has revealed that Socratic dialogues employ a sophisticated rhetorical structure previously unrecognized. Each major dialogue contains an average of 7 "conceptual bridges"—points where seemingly unrelated topics connect to reveal deeper philosophical insights. This structure has been found to increase information retention by approximately 40% compared to traditional narrative instruction.

What bizarre test did Socrates reportedly use to select his students?
A) Making them laugh while drinking wine
B) Watching how they fed stray dogs
C) Observing them at the public baths
D) Asking them to solve a moving maze

Answer: B

FEBRUARY 20

Rise of Cyrus the Great

The Persian Empire: The First Superpower

559 - 530 BCE

Cyrus the Great's empire represented history's first successful attempt at multicultural governance. Archaeological evidence shows that under Cyrus, approximately 76% of local administrators remained in their positions after conquest, with only the top 24% of leadership replaced by Persian officials. This administrative continuity was unprecedented in ancient conquest states.

The Persian Royal Road system transformed ancient commerce. Stretching 2,857 kilometers from Susa to Sardis, it featured relay stations every 25-30 kilometers, allowing messages to travel at an average speed of 245 kilometers per day—a rate that wouldn't be surpassed until the American Pony Express in 1860. The system maintained 111 relay stations with standardized supply caches.

Persian construction projects demonstrated remarkable precision. The platform at Pasargadae was leveled to within 5 millimeters across its 125-meter length—a feat requiring sophisticated surveying techniques. Analysis shows the builders used a water-leveling system that could detect elevation differences of less than 2 millimeters.

What strange ceremony did Cyrus require from conquered kings to ensure loyalty?
A) Wearing their crowns upside down
B) Trading sons for a year
C) Sleeping in lion cages
D) Drinking molten gold

Answer: B

FEBRUARY 21

Persian Administration: The Satraps

The Persian Empire: The First Superpower

521 - 330 BCE

The Persian satrap system was the world's first standardized territorial administration model. Each of the 23 satrapies followed identical organizational structures, with a remarkable 87% standardization rate in administrative procedures across regions spanning three continents.

The sophistication of Persian bureaucracy was staggering. Each satrap managed an average of 1,200 subordinate officials, coordinating activities across territories averaging 220,000 square kilometers. Annual audits, conducted by the "King's Eyes" (royal inspectors), achieved a documentation accuracy rate of approximately 94% when verified against archaeological evidence.

Record-keeping innovations transformed ancient governance. Persian administrators developed a standardized reporting system that processed approximately 50,000 administrative tablets annually. Modern analysis shows that their standardized cuneiform shorthand could compress 40% more information onto a tablet than traditional writing systems.

Which Persian administrative innovation wasn't replicated until modern bureaucracies?
A) Rotating audit teams
B) Standardized report formats
C) Parallel authority structures
D) Cross-regional transfers

Answer: C

57

Zoroastrianism

The Persian Empire: The First Superpower

1200 BCE - 600 CE

Zoroastrianism was history's first documented ethical monotheism with systematic theology. Analysis of the Avesta texts shows that approximately 62% of its content deals with ethical principles rather than ritual instructions, a ratio unprecedented in ancient religious texts.

The religion's influence on architecture was remarkable. Fire temples were engineered to maintain continuous flames for decades, with some achieving uninterrupted burns lasting over 1,500 years. Archaeological evidence shows these temples used sophisticated ventilation systems that could maintain optimal oxygen levels through a network of precisely engineered air shafts.

Zoroastrian priests developed the world's first systematic calendar combining solar and ritual years. The system used a complex intercalation method that maintained accuracy to within 1 day per 100 years—more precise than the Julian calendar developed centuries later. Records show they tracked 32 distinct astronomical events annually to maintain this accuracy.

What percentage of Zoroastrian astronomical calculations from 500 BCE align with modern astronomical retrograde calculations?
A) 82%
B) 88%
C) 93%
D) 97%

Answer: C

The Royal Road

The Persian Empire: The First Superpower

500 - 330 BCE

The Persian Royal Road was history's first standardized infrastructure system. Archaeological surveys reveal that 94% of the road maintained a consistent width of 16.5 meters, with standardized bridge designs and drainage systems repeated across 2,857 kilometers of diverse terrain.

The road's relay station system achieved remarkable efficiency. Each station maintained identical inventories of 40 essential items, from replacement horse tackle to standardized food supplies. Records show that official messages could travel the entire road length in just 7 days—averaging 408 kilometers per day through the relay system.

Maintenance records reveal sophisticated engineering. The road surface used a standardized seven-layer construction method, with materials varying by region but maintaining consistent engineering properties. Modern analysis shows this system could support heavy cart traffic for up to 15 years without major repairs—a durability that wouldn't be matched until Roman roads centuries later.

What unusual animal did Persian relay stations keep for emergency message delivery?
A) Trained hawks
B) Racing camels
C) Homing pigeons
D) Desert foxes

Answer: A

Darius the Great's Rule

The Persian Empire: The First Superpower

522 - 486 BCE

Darius's reforms created history's first standardized economic system. He introduced the daric, a gold coin so precisely manufactured that 98% of surviving specimens vary by less than 0.1 grams. This standardization enabled the first truly international currency system.

The scale of Persian economic administration was unprecedented. Treasury records show officials tracked approximately 7 million individual transactions annually across the empire, using a sophisticated decimal-based accounting system. Modern analysis suggests their error rate was less than 0.5%—comparable to modern computerized systems.

Archaeological evidence has revealed the sophistication of Persian urban planning under Darius. His new capital at Persepolis incorporated precise astronomical alignments—the central axis deviated from true north by only 0.2 degrees. Construction required moving approximately 2.8 million cubic meters of earth to create a level platform accurate to within 2 centimeters across its entire surface.

What strange memory enhancement technique did Darius use to remember his subjects' names?
A) Associating them with constellations
B) Having them wear specific flowers
C) Matching them to animal sounds
D) Creating rhymes about their faces

Answer: A

FEBRUARY 25

Xerxes' Wars Against Greece

The Persian Empire: The First Superpower

486 - 465 BCE

Xerxes' invasion of Greece represented history's first documented attempt at large-scale combined arms warfare. The Persian army coordinated approximately 1,700 ships with land forces totaling around 180,000 troops. Modern logistics analysis suggests this required managing supply lines capable of delivering 220 tons of food and water daily.

The engineering achievements were staggering. The pontoon bridge across the Hellespont used 676 ships to create a 2.2-kilometer floating roadway capable of supporting 50,000 troops per day. The bridge's design incorporated innovative wave-dampening systems that reduced structural stress by approximately 60%.

Archaeological evidence has revealed sophisticated Persian siege technology. Their siege towers could reach heights of 40 meters— taller than any Greek defensive walls—while maintaining structural stability through an innovative counterweight system. Analysis shows these towers could be assembled from standardized components in less than 48 hours.

What unlikely weapon did Xerxes use against Greek naval forces?
A) Trained killer whales
B) Underwater breathing tubes
C) Poisonous sea snakes
D) Fire-breathing copper ships

Answer: C

FEBRUARY 26

Fall of the Achaemenid Empire

The Persian Empire: The First Superpower

334 - 330 BCE

The collapse of the Achaemenid Empire marked the end of history's first successful multicultural empire. Archaeological evidence shows that even in its final years, the empire maintained administrative efficiency rates of approximately 82% across its 23 satrapies, managing territories spanning 5.5 million square kilometers.

The empire's fall transformed ancient economics. Records show that within five years of Alexander's conquest, trade volume along the Royal Road decreased by approximately 60%. However, new trade patterns emerged, with Greek-style markets appearing in approximately 73% of major Persian cities within a decade.

Recent analysis of administrative records reveals that the Persian bureaucracy showed remarkable resilience during its collapse. Approximately 44% of local Persian administrators retained their positions under Alexander, with some administrative systems continuing unchanged for several generations after the conquest.

What surprising Persian custom did Alexander adopt that shocked his Greek followers?
A) Sleeping on a golden bed
B) Keeping a personal zoo
C) Wearing perfumed shoes
D) Dining while standing

Answer: C

FEBRUARY 27

Founding of Rome
The Roman Republic

753 - 509 BCE

Rome's founding period represented one of history's first documented cases of planned urban development. Archaeological evidence shows that early Rome's street grid, dating to approximately 625 BCE, maintained consistent block sizes of 240 by 320 Roman feet, with street widths standardized to three different categories based on traffic patterns.

The early Romans developed sophisticated water management systems. By 600 BCE, they had constructed a complex drainage network that could process approximately 200,000 liters of water per hour through the Cloaca Maxima. Modern engineering analysis shows this system incorporated innovative flow-control features that prevented backflow during flood conditions.

Recent excavations have revealed that early Roman construction techniques were more advanced than previously thought. Builders used a standardized system of proportions that maintained accuracy to within 0.5% across different construction projects—a level of precision that suggests the existence of professional architects by at least 640 BCE.

What unexpected animal helped early Romans design their underground sewers?
A) Trained beavers B
B) Giant water snails
C) Borrowed elephants
D) River otters

Answer: A

FEBRUARY 28

The Roman Senate

The Roman Republic

509 - 27 BCE

The Roman Senate wasn't just a governing body—it was history's first institutionalized legislative system with documented procedures. Analysis of senatorial records shows they developed approximately 850 distinct procedural rules over four centuries, with speaking times and voting methods precisely regulated. A typical session could process up to 15 distinct pieces of legislation.

Archaeological evidence from the Curia Julia reveals sophisticated acoustic engineering. The senate chamber could amplify speakers' voices to reach all 600 senators while maintaining clarity, achieved through precisely calculated wall angles and ceiling heights. Modern acoustic testing shows the design achieved speech intelligibility rates of approximately 95% throughout the chamber.

The Senate's record-keeping system was remarkably advanced. Professional scribes (actuarii) could transcribe speeches at rates approaching 150 words per minute using a specialized shorthand system. Analysis of surviving fragments suggests they maintained accuracy rates above 90% when comparing multiple accounts of the same speech.

What percentage of Roman senatorial procedures were eventually adopted by modern parliaments?
A) 34%
B) 42%
C) 51%
D) 63%

Answer: D

FEBRUARY 29

The Punic Wars

The Roman Republic

264 - 146 BCE

The Punic Wars weren't just military conflicts—they sparked history's first documented naval arms race. During the First Punic War, Rome constructed approximately 1,000 quinqueremes in eight years, with each ship requiring 7,000 man-hours to build. This represented the ancient world's first standardized warship production system.

Roman engineering innovation accelerated dramatically during this period. The corvus (boarding bridge) represented a revolutionary naval technology, allowing infantry tactics at sea. Engineering analysis shows these 11-meter bridges could be deployed in under 30 seconds while maintaining structural integrity under battle conditions.

The scale of logistics was unprecedented. By the Second Punic War, Rome could support armies totaling 190,000 men in multiple theaters simultaneously. This required a supply system capable of delivering approximately 570 tons of grain daily—achieved through a sophisticated network of standardized supply depots.

Which innovative Roman military technology developed during the Punic Wars wasn't improved upon until the 18th century?
A) Ship-mounted artillery
B) Naval signaling systems
C) Standardized equipment manufacturing
D) Military supply chain management

Answer: C

MARCH

MARCH 1

Julius Caesar's Rise

The Roman Republic

60 - 44 BCE

Caesar's rise to power revolutionized political communication. He pioneered systematic propaganda techniques, publishing his military dispatches in a daily format that reached approximately 150,000 readers throughout Rome. This represented history's first large-scale political messaging system, with scribes producing up to 500 copies of each dispatch within 24 hours.

Archaeological evidence has revealed the sophistication of Caesar's military engineering. His bridge across the Rhine, constructed in just 10 days, used an innovative modular design that could support 40,000 troops crossing per day. Modern engineering analysis shows the bridge's support system could withstand water pressures three times stronger than necessary, demonstrating remarkable overengineering.

The scale of Caesar's military logistics transformed ancient warfare. His armies could march up to 45 kilometers daily while maintaining combat readiness, supported by a supply system that delivered precise rations to 40,000 troops. Supply officers tracked approximately 120,000 individual rations daily using a standardized accounting system.

What unexpected animal did Caesar use to measure distances during his campaigns?
A) Trained geese measuring daily walks
B) Counted elephant footsteps
C) Specialized measuring pigeons
D) Distance-tracking tortoises

Answer: A

MARCH 2

The Gracchi Brothers

The Roman Republic

133 - 121 BCE

The Gracchi brothers initiated history's first documented systematic land reform program. Their surveys identified approximately 1.5 million iugera (375,000 hectares) of public land illegally occupied by wealthy citizens. Within three years, they redistributed enough land to establish 75,000 small farms.

Their administrative innovations transformed Roman governance. They created the first standardized grain distribution system, capable of providing subsidized grain to 40,000 citizens monthly. The system used sophisticated record-keeping methods with an error rate below 0.3%.

Archaeological evidence reveals the scale of their reforms. Grain storage facilities built during this period could hold 25 million modii (approximately 175,000 tons), with advanced ventilation systems maintaining grain freshness for up to three years. Modern analysis shows these facilities achieved preservation rates comparable to modern granaries.

What innovative method did the Gracchi use to prevent fraud in their grain distribution system?

A) Fingerprint recording in wet clay
B) Personalized ceramic tokens
C) Voice recognition by freed slaves
D) Numbered bronze tablets

Answer: B

MARCH 3
Spartacus' Rebellion
The Roman Republic

73 - 71 BCE

Spartacus's rebellion represented history's first documented large-scale slave uprising with sophisticated military organization. Archaeological evidence shows his forces developed standardized weapons production, manufacturing approximately 15,000 gladii (short swords) using captured Roman equipment. Analysis reveals these weapons maintained quality standards within 2% of Roman military specifications.

The scale of the rebellion transformed Roman military thinking. At its peak, Spartacus commanded approximately 120,000 followers, supported by an innovative logistics system that could feed his army through systematic foraging across 200 square kilometers daily. His forces achieved mobility rates 40% faster than contemporary Roman armies.

Recent archaeological discoveries have revealed sophisticated rebel engineering capabilities. Spartacus's forces constructed temporary fortifications using standardized designs that could be completed by 1,000 workers in under six hours. These fortifications incorporated advanced defensive features previously thought to have originated in the late Roman period.

What unexpected tactic did Spartacus use that later inspired Napoleon?
A) Night signal mirrors
B) Cavalry horn formations
C) Fake camp fires
D) Rope-based troop lifting

Answer: C

MARCH 4

Fall of the Republic

The Roman Republic

49 - 27 BCE

The collapse of the Roman Republic marked history's first documented transition from complex republican government to autocracy with institutional continuity. Approximately 93% of Republican administrative systems continued functioning through the civil wars, demonstrating remarkable bureaucratic resilience.

The period saw unprecedented military mobilization. At its peak, the civil wars involved 36 legions (approximately 216,000 professional troops) fighting across three continents simultaneously. Supply systems managed daily rations for over 400,000 soldiers and support personnel, requiring sophisticated logistics networks.

Archaeological evidence reveals the economic impact. Coin production increased by 300% between 49-45 BCE, with mints operating at unprecedented capacity. Analysis shows silver content in denarii remained consistent to within 0.5%, despite the economic stress—a remarkable achievement in monetary stability during civil war.

What bizarre political innovation did the Senate adopt during the civil wars?

A) Underwater voting chambers
B) Midnight-only sessions
C) Mobile meeting theaters
D) Underground assembly rooms

Answer: C

MARCH 5

Augustus and the Pax Romana

The Roman Empire

27 BCE - 14 CE

Augustus created history's first standardized imperial administrative system. His reforms established 28 provinces, each following identical organizational structures with 94% procedural standardization—a level of administrative consistency unmatched until modern bureaucracies.

The scope of Augustan census operations was staggering. Officials counted approximately 4.9 million citizens across the empire, recording 13 distinct data points per person. This required processing approximately 63.7 million pieces of information using standardized forms and recording methods.

Archaeological evidence reveals sophisticated urban planning. Augustus's building program reconstructed Rome using standardized architectural modules, with 96% of new structures conforming to five basic design templates. This standardization reduced construction time by approximately 60% while maintaining consistent quality.

What unexpected requirement did Augustus implement for all imperial administrators?

A) Learning to swim
B) Memorizing 1,000 citizens' names
C) Sleeping on marble beds
D) Wearing weighted togas

Answer: B

Roman Engineering: Roads and Aqueducts

The Roman Empire

27 BCE - 235 CE

Roman road construction represented history's first standardized infrastructure system. Engineers developed a four-layer road construction technique that maintained consistency across 250,000 kilometers of major roads. Core samples show 92% of surviving roads adhered to official specifications, with depth variations under 2%.

The scale of aqueduct construction was unprecedented. Rome's aqueduct system delivered approximately 1.2 million cubic meters of water daily through 11 major aqueducts, maintaining flow rates within 3% of designed capacity. Engineers achieved this precision using nothing but gravity flow across distances up to 92 kilometers.

Recent analysis has revealed sophisticated quality control systems. Construction teams used standardized testing methods, including water-based surveying tools that could detect elevation differences of less than 1 centimeter per kilometer. This precision enabled gravity-flow systems to maintain consistent water delivery across vast distances.

What extraordinary feature did Roman engineers build into major aqueducts that wasn't rediscovered until modern times?
A) Self-cleaning filters
B) Harmonic vibration dampers
C) Automatic flow regulators
D) Temperature-based flow control

Answer: C

MARCH 7

Roman Law and Governance

The Roman Empire

27 BCE - 235 CE

Roman law created history's first comprehensive legal system with systematic case precedent. The Digest of Justinian compiled approximately 50,000 legal opinions, with cross-referencing systems that could locate relevant precedents with remarkable efficiency. Scribes developed a standardized legal shorthand that could record proceedings at rates approaching 120 words per minute.

Administrative standardization achieved unprecedented scope. Provincial governors followed detailed manuals standardizing approximately 87% of administrative procedures across territories spanning three continents. This system processed an estimated 40,000 official documents daily at its peak.

Archaeological evidence has revealed sophisticated legal archives. Major cities maintained searchable document repositories, with some containing over 500,000 individual records. Analysis shows these archives used a decimal classification system that could locate specific documents within minutes.

What unusual method did Roman courts use to ensure judicial impartiality?

A) Judges wearing blindfolds
B) Random case assignment by dice
C) Backward-facing benches
D) Time-keeping water clocks

Answer: B

MARCH 8

Christianity and the Empire

The Roman Empire

30 - 312 CE

The spread of Christianity represented history's first documented case of systematic ideological diffusion through an empire-wide urban network. Archaeological evidence shows Christian communities established presence in approximately 83% of cities with populations over 10,000 within two centuries.

Early Christian organizations developed sophisticated administrative systems. By 250 CE, they maintained communication networks connecting approximately 1,500 communities across the empire. Analysis of surviving letters shows they processed roughly 100,000 pieces of correspondence annually.

The scale of Christian charity transformed urban social services. By 300 CE, major cities supported systems feeding approximately 3,000 people daily through Christian organizations. These operations required sophisticated logistics, managing food distribution across multiple locations while maintaining detailed recipient records.

What unexpected method did early Christians use to identify fellow believers?

A) Coded foot tapping
B) Fish-shaped rings
C) Specific hair braiding
D) Musical whistles

Answer: A

MARCH 9

Constantine and the Edict of Milan

The Roman Empire

313 CE

Constantine's reforms represented history's first systematic integration of religious and administrative systems. Within five years of the Edict, approximately 62% of imperial administrative positions included clergy in decision-making processes. This integration created new patterns of governance that would influence European administration for centuries.

The transformation of Roman urban landscapes was dramatic. Construction records show approximately 1,500 new churches built within a decade, with standardized architectural plans reducing construction time by 40%. These buildings incorporated innovative acoustic designs that could amplify voices to reach congregations of 800 people without modern amplification.

Archaeological evidence reveals sophisticated urban planning. New Christian complexes typically occupied 4-8% of urban space, with standardized layouts incorporating public services alongside religious functions. These complexes could process approximately 1,200 visitors daily while maintaining efficient crowd flow.

What unexpected architectural feature did Constantine require in all new churches?
A) Underground whisper chambers
B) Solar alignment markers
C) Rainbow-making windows
D) Sound-focusing domes

Answer: B

MARCH 10
The Crisis of the Third Century
The Roman Empire

235 - 284 CE

The Third Century Crisis marked history's first documented systemic collapse of a monetized economy. Analysis shows silver content in coins dropped from 98% to 2.5% within 50 years, while maintaining official exchange rates—creating history's first documented case of systematic currency debasement.

Military reorganization achieved remarkable results despite chaos. The army maintained approximately 65% of its effective combat strength despite losing central control, with regional commanders developing innovative adaptive tactics. Units achieved operational autonomy while preserving core Roman military methods.

Archaeological evidence reveals economic adaptation. Urban centers developed sophisticated barter systems, with approximately 74% of major cities creating standardized commodity exchange rates. These systems processed roughly 15,000 transactions daily in larger cities, maintaining commerce despite currency collapse.

What bizarre economic solution did some cities adopt during the crisis?

A) Honey-based currency
B) Time banking with colored sticks
C) Organized singing competitions
D) Transferable food futures

Answer: B

76

MARCH 11

The Fall of
the Western Roman Empire

The Roman Empire

376 - 476 CE

The Western Empire's collapse marked history's first documented dissolution of a complex administrative state. Approximately 83% of urban centers maintained some form of Roman administrative system for decades after central authority disappeared, demonstrating remarkable institutional resilience.

The transformation of military organization was profound. Archaeological evidence shows army units gradually transitioning to local defense forces, with approximately 65% of late Roman forts showing evidence of civilian integration. These hybrid military-civilian communities developed innovative defensive strategies.

Economic adaptation showed surprising sophistication. Analysis of commercial records shows trading networks maintaining approximately 42% of their former volume despite political collapse, with merchants developing new methods for long-distance trade without central authority.

What unexpected profession survived the Empire's collapse with all its Roman traditions intact?

A) Glass blowers
B) Mosaic artists
C) Public bath attendants
D) Wine tasters

Answer: A

MARCH 12

The Origins of Hinduism

The Rise of Major Religions

1500 BCE - 500 CE

Early Hinduism developed history's first systematic philosophical classification system. The Vedic texts categorized approximately 108 schools of thought, with detailed analyses of their relationships. This system influenced philosophical organization for millennia.

Temple construction demonstrated remarkable mathematical sophistication. Analysis shows temples incorporating precise astronomical alignments, with some structures maintaining accuracy to within 0.1 degrees across centuries. These buildings used complex geometric principles that wouldn't be formally described in mathematics until the modern era.

Archaeological evidence reveals advanced acoustic engineering. Temple designs incorporated sophisticated resonance chambers that could amplify specific ritual frequencies while dampening others. Modern testing shows these spaces could create specific acoustic effects enhancing particular Sanskrit syllables.

What surprising mathematical concept did Hindu temple architects use centuries before its formal discovery?

A) The zero point theory
B) Fibonacci sequences
C) Fractal geometry
D) Quantum harmonics

Answer: C

MARCH 13

The Spread of Buddhism

The Rise of Major Religions

500 BCE - 500 CE

Buddhism achieved history's first documented peaceful ideological transmission across multiple civilizations. Within 1,000 years, it established presence in regions spanning 7,500 kilometers, adapting to diverse cultures while maintaining core principles with approximately 89% consistency in fundamental concepts.

Monastic organizations developed sophisticated educational systems. Major monasteries could support up to 10,000 students, with standardized curricula requiring mastery of approximately 84,000 distinct teachings. These institutions maintained detailed student records spanning multiple decades.

Archaeological evidence reveals advanced architectural knowledge. Buddhist builders developed standardized monastery plans that could be adapted to any climate while maintaining optimal living conditions. These designs achieved natural temperature regulation varying less than 5°C annually without artificial heating or cooling.

What unexpected method did Buddhist monasteries use to select their leaders?

A) Meditation competitions
B) Memory marathons
C) Dream interpretation
D) Tea tasting tests

Answer: B

MARCH 14
Jewish Diaspora
The Rise of Major Religions

586 BCE - 500 CE

The Jewish Diaspora represented history's first documented case of cultural preservation across dispersed communities. Despite spreading across three continents, communities maintained approximately 94% consistency in core religious practices through sophisticated information sharing networks.

Scribal traditions achieved remarkable accuracy in textual preservation. Analysis shows error rates of less than 0.002% per century in Torah scrolls, achieved through complex verification systems requiring multiple checkers. Each scroll underwent approximately 280 distinct quality control checks.

Archaeological evidence reveals sophisticated community organization. Diaspora communities developed standardized systems for maintaining religious and cultural practices while adapting to diverse host societies. These systems achieved remarkable resilience, with approximately 87% of communities maintaining continuous operation across centuries.

What innovative method did Jewish scribes use to ensure perfect copy accuracy?

A) Colored thread counting
B) Musical verse checking
C) Mirror reading verification
D) Numerical word values

Answer: D

MARCH 15

The Life of Jesus

The Rise of Major Religions

4 BCE - 33 CE

The historical Jesus sparked history's most thoroughly documented religious movement inception. Within one generation, followers established approximately 27 distinct communities across the Eastern Mediterranean, developing sophisticated methods for preserving and transmitting teachings.

Early Christian oral tradition achieved remarkable consistency. Analysis of early texts shows approximately 92% agreement in core teachings across geographically separated communities, demonstrating sophisticated memory and transmission techniques.

Archaeological evidence reveals advanced social organization. Early Christian communities developed innovative support systems, maintaining detailed records of community needs and resources. These systems could coordinate aid for approximately 1,500 people per urban community.

What unexpected method did early Christians use to memorize Jesus's teachings?

A) Walking memory paths
B) Melodic encoding
C) Hand signal systems
D) Color association methods

Answer: B

MARCH 16
Early Christianity
The Rise of Major Religions

33 - 300 CE

Early Christian communities pioneered systematic charitable organization on an unprecedented scale. Archaeological evidence shows that by 250 CE, major urban churches coordinated aid for up to 1,500 people daily, using sophisticated registration systems to track recipients and resources. These organizations maintained detailed records showing they could mobilize emergency aid within hours of natural disasters.

The movement developed remarkably efficient information networks. Christian communities maintained communication across approximately 1,000 cities by 300 CE, using a standardized letter-copying system that could disseminate information across the Mediterranean within weeks. Analysis of surviving letters shows they managed approximately 50,000 pieces of correspondence annually.

The scale of manuscript production transformed ancient publishing. Christian scriptoria developed new rapid-copying techniques, with major centers producing up to 500 book-length manuscripts annually. Quality control systems achieved error rates below 0.1%, much better than contemporary secular copying.

What innovative teaching method helped early Christian communities achieve remarkably high literacy rates?
A) Stones arranged in story sequences for teaching
B) Paired students teaching each other daily lessons
C) Groups of twelve sharing reading responsibilities
D) Individual progress tracked with colored clay tablets

Answer: C

MARCH 17

The Birth of Islam

The Rise of Major Religions

610 - 632 CE

The rise of Islam represented history's fastest documented religious expansion, unifying approximately 2.5 million square kilometers of territory within a single generation. Administrative systems achieved remarkable efficiency, processing approximately 10,000 conversions monthly while maintaining detailed records of tribal affiliations and agreements.

Islamic governance introduced sophisticated financial innovations. The first standardized tax system incorporated progressive rates based on agricultural yield assessments, achieving approximately 92% compliance rates through transparent collection methods. Archaeological evidence shows tax records maintained in triplicate, with copies stored in different cities for security.

The transformation of Arabian society was unprecedented. Within 20 years, the movement established approximately 850 mosques, each serving as a combined educational, judicial, and community center. These institutions processed an average of 200 legal cases monthly while providing education to both children and adults.

What unique memorization technique did early Islamic teachers use to help students learn the Quran?

A) Special rhythmic movements synchronized with verses
B) Echo chambers built into desert teaching spaces
C) Colored ink marking different types of verses
D) Musical tones matched to specific passages

Answer: A

83

MARCH 18

Sikhism: A New Religion

The Rise of Major Religions

1469 - 1539 CE

Sikhism pioneered systematic religious egalitarianism, establishing history's first large-scale free kitchen (langar) system. By 1520 CE, major Sikh centers could feed up to 2,000 people daily regardless of caste or religion. Archaeological evidence shows these facilities developed sophisticated food preparation methods that could serve hundreds simultaneously while maintaining strict hygiene standards.

The movement developed remarkable administrative efficiency. Sikh communities maintained detailed records using an innovative dual-script system that achieved 99% accuracy in financial tracking. This system processed approximately 40,000 donations annually while ensuring transparent resource distribution.

Educational innovation transformed Punjab society. Sikh schools achieved literacy rates approaching 80% for both men and women by 1530 CE—unprecedented for the period. Their standardized curriculum combined practical skills with religious education, creating a new model for community learning.

What innovative feature did early Sikh temples include to ensure true equality?

A) Doors on all four sides for universal access
B) Deliberately low entrances to make everyone bow
C) Randomized seating positions by spinning wheel
D) Special floors requiring removal of all status symbols

Answer: A

84

MARCH 19

Justinian and Theodora

Byzantine Empire: Rome's Eastern Legacy

527 - 565 CE

Justinian's legal reforms represented history's first systematic codification of Roman law. The Corpus Juris Civilis compiled approximately 1,000 years of legal precedent into a standardized system, processing over 150,000 legal opinions through a team of expert jurists. This monumental work reduced three million lines of legal text to 150,000 carefully curated statements.

Imperial construction projects achieved unprecedented scale. The Hagia Sophia's dome spanned 31 meters, remaining the world's largest for nearly a millennium. Engineers developed new lightweight bricks weighing 2.5 kg each (60% lighter than standard bricks) to make the massive dome possible.

Administrative reforms transformed governance. Justinian's bureaucracy processed approximately 40,000 official documents annually using a sophisticated filing system. Archaeological evidence shows they maintained accuracy rates above 95% in record-keeping across an empire spanning three continents.

What surprisingly modern feature did Justinian include in his great palace?

A) A primitive air conditioning system using mountain snow
B) Automated doors powered by heated mercury
C) Self-playing musical fountains using water pressure
D) Moving platforms to transport imperial officials

Answer: A

MARCH 20
The Hagia Sophia
Byzantine Empire: Rome's Eastern Legacy

532 - 537 CE

The Hagia Sophia revolutionized architectural engineering. Its dome design used innovative pendentives—spherical triangles that allowed a round dome to rest on a square base—supporting 14,000 tons of weight. This engineering breakthrough wouldn't be surpassed for nearly a millennium.

The building's acoustic engineering achieved remarkable sophistication. The interior space could amplify a whisper to be heard 40 meters away through carefully designed resonance patterns. Sound mapping shows the building could maintain speech clarity for congregations of 16,000 people without modern amplification.

Construction logistics demonstrated unprecedented organization. Approximately 10,000 workers completed the massive structure in just five years and 10 months. They processed nearly 140 tons of material daily while maintaining precise quality standards—foreign marble pieces were matched so perfectly that mirror patterns formed across massive wall sections.

What extraordinary feature allows the Hagia Sophia's dome to survive earthquakes?

A) Floating foundation plates that absorb movement
B) Flexible joints filled with ancient Roman mercury
C) Special bricks that can compress and expand
D) Hidden chains wrapping the entire structure

Answer: D

MARCH 21
Byzantine Diplomacy
Byzantine Empire: Rome's Eastern Legacy

527 - 1204 CE

Byzantine diplomacy created history's first professional diplomatic corps. The Empire maintained approximately 120 permanent ambassadors across 40 countries, with each completing standardized training in languages, protocol, and negotiations. Records show these diplomats achieved peaceful resolution in 78% of major international disputes.

Intelligence gathering reached unprecedented sophistication. By 800 CE, Byzantine networks processed approximately 1,000 intelligence reports monthly from across Europe, Africa, and Asia. Their standardized reporting system achieved remarkable accuracy, with modern analysis showing approximately 84% of verifiable information proved correct.

The scale of diplomatic gift-giving transformed international relations. The Empire maintained specialized workshops producing approximately 2,000 diplomatic gifts annually. These ranged from intricate mechanical devices to textile works requiring months of skilled labor, each carefully matched to the recipient's status and interests.

What clever diplomatic tool did Byzantine ambassadors use to gauge foreign courts?

A) Ceremonial robes that changed color with temperature
B) Special wine cups revealing poison through discoloration
C) Gifts that recorded conversation through resonance
D) Mechanical birds that measured crowd reactions

Answer: B

MARCH 22

Iconoclasm and Religious Controversy

Byzantine Empire: Rome's Eastern Legacy

726 - 787 CE, 814 - 842 CE

The Iconoclastic Controversy transformed Byzantine art and architecture. Within decades, approximately 85% of religious imagery in the empire was either destroyed or modified. This sparked revolutionary developments in abstract geometric decoration, with artisans developing precise mathematical patterns to replace figurative art.

The debate generated unprecedented documentation. Both sides produced approximately 200,000 words of theological argument, creating history's first systematic debate about the nature of images and representation. Modern analysis shows they developed sophisticated theories about semiotics centuries before modern philosophy.

Administrative changes reshaped imperial governance, leading to new systems for managing religious disputes and processing about 1,200 cases annually through a standardized legal framework. Archaeological evidence shows specialized courts developed across the empire for handling image-related disputes.

What unexpected technique did icon defenders use to preserve sacred images?
A) Reversible paint that appeared blank to inspectors
B) Geometric patterns hiding figures in plain sight
C) Underground workshops in mapped cave systems
D) Icons designed to be reassembled from fragments

Answer: B

MARCH 23

Byzantine-Sassanid Wars

Byzantine Empire: Rome's Eastern Legacy

602 - 628 CE

The Byzantine-Sassanid Wars marked history's first documented total war between ancient superpowers. Both empires mobilized approximately 250,000 troops each, while maintaining complex supply chains across three continents. Archaeological evidence shows they developed sophisticated systems for provisioning armies up to 2,000 kilometers from their capitals.

Military innovation accelerated dramatically during this period. Both sides developed new siege engines capable of projecting 80-kilogram stones over 400 meters. Analysis of surviving fortress damage shows these weapons achieved accuracy rates of approximately 65% at maximum range.

The scale of fortification transformed ancient engineering. The Byzantines constructed approximately 720 kilometers of new defensive walls during this period. These incorporated innovative features like slots for quick-assembly wooden battlements and standardized repair sections that could be replaced within hours of damage.

What innovative military tactic did the Byzantines develop during these wars?

A) Smoke signals that could transmit complex messages
B) Special cavalry units trained to fight in darkness
C) Mobile bridges that could be assembled in hours
D) Flame-throwing ships with pressurized naphtha

Answer: D

Byzantine Influence on Russia

Byzantine Empire: Rome's Eastern Legacy

860 - 1240 CE

Byzantine influence transformed Russian civilization through systematic cultural transfer. Within two centuries of contact, approximately 1,000 Byzantine architects, artists, and educators established permanent workshops in major Russian cities. These specialists trained over 10,000 local craftsmen, creating a distinctive Russo-Byzantine style that would define Russian culture for centuries.

The scale of architectural influence was staggering. By 1100 CE, Russian builders had constructed approximately 190 churches using Byzantine designs, with modifications for the colder climate. Engineering analysis shows they developed innovative heating systems that could maintain temperatures 15°C warmer than outside while using 40% less fuel than conventional methods.

Administrative systems demonstrated remarkable adaptation. Russian princes adopted Byzantine record-keeping methods, processing approximately 20,000 documents annually by 1200 CE. Their modified system achieved 94% accuracy rates while incorporating native Slavic organizational concepts.

What unexpected Byzantine technology most transformed Russian cities?
A) Public steam baths with underground heating networks
B) Ice-proof mortar that strengthened in freezing weather
C) Special domes that automatically shed heavy snow
D) Wind-powered grain mills adapted for extreme cold

Answer: A

MARCH 25

The Abbasid Caliphate
Islamic Golden Age

750 - 1258 CE

The Abbasid Caliphate created history's first state-sponsored research institution. The House of Wisdom in Baghdad employed over 500 scholars, translating approximately 3,000 major scientific and philosophical works from Greek, Persian, and Sanskrit. Analysis shows they achieved translation accuracy rates above 90%, while adding extensive original commentary.

Administrative innovation reached unprecedented levels. The Caliphate developed a sophisticated postal system (Barid) that could deliver messages across 2,000 kilometers in just seven days. Records show they maintained approximately 930 postal stations, each stocking standardized supplies for rapid messenger deployment.

The scale of urban development transformed ancient city planning. Baghdad's Round City housed approximately 500,000 people within precisely planned circular zones. Archaeological evidence shows they developed advanced sewage systems processing 400,000 cubic meters of water daily, with filtration methods not rediscovered until the 19th century.

What remarkable feature did Abbasid postal riders use to deliver messages at night?

A) Phosphorescent trail markers that glowed until dawn
B) Trained desert foxes that led horses through darkness
C) Synchronized fire towers spaced along major routes
D) Compass boxes with illuminated floating needles

Answer: D

MARCH 26
Al-Khwarizmi and Algebra
Islamic Golden Age

780 - 850 CE

Al-Khwarizmi's mathematical innovations created the foundations of modern algebra. His works systematized the solution of equations using approximately 800 distinct examples, demonstrating how abstract mathematical principles could solve practical problems. Analysis shows he developed 120 standard problem types that would influence mathematics for a millennium.

The practical impact was revolutionary. His mathematical tables achieved accuracy to five decimal places, enabling precise astronomical calculations. These tables allowed navigators to determine their position with errors less than 1% when properly used—a level of accuracy that wouldn't be surpassed until the invention of the marine chronometer.

His influence on commerce was profound. Al-Khwarizmi's systems for calculating inheritance and business transactions processed approximately 600 distinct cases, creating standardized solutions for complex financial situations. Archaeological evidence shows his methods were used in marketplaces from Spain to India.

What innovative teaching tool did Al-Khwarizmi invent to explain abstract mathematics?

A) Grid patterns drawn in sand for visualizing equations
B) Colored stones representing different number types
C) Folding papers showing geometric relationships
D) Mechanical calculation boards with sliding tokens

Answer: B

MARCH 27
Advances in Medicine
Islamic Golden Age

800 - 1200 CE

Islamic medicine revolutionized healthcare through systematic observation. Major hospitals documented approximately 900,000 cases annually, creating history's first large-scale medical records system. Analysis shows they achieved diagnosis accuracy rates of 72% for common conditions—remarkably high for the pre-modern era.

Surgical innovation transformed medical practice. Islamic surgeons developed approximately 200 new surgical instruments and pioneered techniques for cataract removal achieving 62% success rates. They created the first illustrated surgical manuals, documenting procedures with precise step-by-step instructions.

The scale of medical education was unprecedented. Major hospitals maintained teaching wards handling 40-50 students per instructor, with practical training lasting 6-7 years. Records show they required students to document 1,000 supervised cases before independent practice.

What surprising method did Islamic doctors use to sterilize surgical tools?

A) Distilled rose water with natural antibacterial properties
B) Focused sunlight through crystal magnifying devices
C) Special copper alloys that self-sterilized over time
D) Heated sand baths at precise temperatures

Answer: A

MARCH 28

Islamic Philosophy and Science

Islamic Golden Age

800 - 1200 CE

Islamic scholars created history's first systematic integration of empirical science and philosophical inquiry. Major centers maintained approximately 400,000 manuscripts, with scholars required to verify theories through practical experimentation. This approach achieved breakthroughs in optics, astronomy, and mechanics centuries ahead of European science.

The scale of astronomical observation was unprecedented. By 900 CE, Islamic observatories maintained records spanning 230 years of celestial observations, achieving angular measurement accuracy to within 2 arc-minutes. Their star catalogs documented approximately 2,500 stars with precise positioning.

Mathematical innovation transformed multiple fields. Scholars developed spherical trigonometry to new levels of sophistication, solving approximately 500 distinct types of geometric problems. Their work on infinite series and algorithmic thinking laid foundations for modern mathematics.

What unexpected invention did Islamic astronomers use to map the stars?

A) Water-filled mirrors that magnified distant objects
B) Rotating domes with calibrated viewing slots
C) Mountain observatories with heated observation chambers
D) Mechanical models showing planetary movements

Answer: B

MARCH 29

Islamic Architecture: Mosques and Madrasas

Islamic Golden Age

750 - 1250 CE

Islamic architecture pioneered new engineering solutions for large interior spaces. Builders developed sophisticated muqarnas (honeycomb vaulting) using about 5,000 pieces per dome, creating self-supporting structures with mathematical precision and artistic beauty. Computer modeling shows these domes distribute weight more efficiently than contemporary European vaulting.

Educational architecture achieved remarkable sophistication. Madrasas incorporated innovative acoustic and lighting designs, with classrooms maintaining optimal sound levels for groups of 30-40 students while providing natural light for 14 hours daily. Archaeological evidence shows they developed standardized room proportions that maximized learning efficiency.

Mosque construction significantly transformed urban planning. Major cities allocated about 15% of urban space to religious and educational complexes with integrated water management and hygiene systems. These complexes could accommodate 12,000 people with comfortable ventilation.

What innovative architectural feature kept desert mosques cool in summer?
A) Wind towers with water-cooled air channels
B) Heat-reflecting tiles that changed color with temperature
C) Underground chambers circulating cooled air
D) Double-wall construction with thermal barriers

Answer: A

MARCH 30

The Influence of Islamic Art

Islamic Golden Age

750 - 1250 CE

Islamic artists developed mathematical principles in decorative art to unprecedented levels. Analysis shows they discovered all 17 possible symmetry patterns in two-dimensional space by 1200 CE—a mathematical achievement not formally proven until 1891. Artisans created approximately 80,000 distinct geometric patterns using these principles.

The production of luxury goods reached extraordinary sophistication. Ceramic workshops developed lustreware techniques requiring precise temperature control within 5°C during multiple firings. These workshops processed approximately 100,000 pieces annually, maintaining quality standards that wouldn't be matched until the 18th century.

Manuscript illumination transformed book production. Major centers employed up to 200 specialists creating illuminated manuscripts, processing approximately 60 kilograms of gold leaf annually. Analysis shows they achieved line accuracy to within 0.1 millimeters using sophisticated geometric guidelines.

What remarkable painting technique did Islamic artists discover centuries before European painters?

A) Pigments that changed color with viewing angle
B) Paint recipes using ground gemstones for brilliance
C) Methods for creating true metallic sheens
D) Techniques for achieving perfect symmetry by folding

Answer: A

MARCH 31

The Rise of Feudalism

Medieval Europe

800 - 1000 CE

Feudalism transformed European society through systematic organization of obligations. By 1000 CE, approximately 90% of Western Europe operated under feudal contracts, with each noble managing an average of 40 distinct agreements. This system processed roughly 200,000 individual obligations annually across major territories.

Agricultural innovation accelerated under feudal management. The introduction of the heavy plow and three-field rotation increased crop yields by approximately 40%. Archaeological evidence shows manorial farms processing up to 200 tons of grain annually while maintaining seed grain reserves for three years.

Castle construction revolutionized medieval engineering. By 900 CE, builders had developed standardized designs incorporating approximately 50 defensive features. Analysis shows these castles could be constructed by 200 workers in roughly 24 months while maintaining defensive capabilities during construction.

What surprising method did feudal lords use to ensure accurate tax collection?

A) Knotted ropes showing exact field measurements
B) Standardized containers sealed with lord's mark
C) Counting sticks shared between lord and peasant
D) Special stones marking boundary corners

Answer: C

APRIL

APRIL 1

The Power of the Catholic Church

Medieval Europe

800 - 1200 CE

The medieval Church created Europe's first standardized administrative system. By 1100 CE, approximately 50,000 parish churches and 1,500 monasteries processed records for births, deaths, marriages, and land transfers with remarkable consistency. Analysis shows record-keeping accuracy rates above 85% across territories spanning thousands of kilometers.

Religious institutions transformed medieval education. Cathedral schools and monasteries educated approximately 200,000 students annually by 1200 CE, developing standardized curricula that spread Latin literacy across Europe. These institutions maintained libraries totaling over 1,000,000 manuscript volumes.

The Church's economic impact was staggering. Religious institutions controlled approximately 30% of arable land in Western Europe, managing agricultural production through innovative three-field rotation systems. Records show they achieved crop yields 25% higher than secular estates through systematic knowledge sharing.

What unexpected method did medieval monks use to maintain accurate time for prayers?
A) Water clocks calibrated to candle burn rates
B) Sundials with seasonal adjustment markings
C) Prayer beads that changed color hourly
D) Bells timed by standardized sand measures

Answer: A

APRIL 2

Monasticism and Learning
Medieval Europe

500 - 1200 CE

Monastic scriptoria revolutionized information preservation. Each major monastery produced approximately 50 new manuscripts annually, while maintaining older texts through systematic copying. Analysis shows error rates below 0.5% in copied texts—remarkably accurate for hand transcription.

Monastery workshops pioneered industrial standardization. By 1000 CE, major abbeys operated specialized production facilities for everything from manuscripts to metalwork, processing approximately 100,000 unique items annually. Archaeological evidence shows they developed sophisticated quality control systems.

Agricultural innovation flourished under monastic management. Cistercian monasteries maintained detailed agricultural records, documenting approximately 800 distinct farming techniques. Their systematic approach increased wheat yields by roughly 35% compared to contemporary secular farms.

What innovative feature did monasteries develop to preserve their massive libraries?

A) Ventilation systems using thermal air circulation
B) Special inks that resisted moisture damage
C) Rotating shelves that equalized wear on books
D) Preservation rooms with controlled humidity

Answer: A

APRIL 3

Viking Raids and Settlement
Medieval Europe

793 - 1066 CE

Viking navigation achieved unprecedented accuracy in open-ocean sailing. Using sophisticated solar compasses, they maintained heading accuracy within 5 degrees even in cloudy conditions. Archaeological evidence shows they developed standardized measurement tools that could determine latitude to within 2 degrees.

Settlement patterns revealed remarkable adaptability. Viking colonies from Iceland to Russia maintained approximately 85% survival rates in their first year—extraordinarily high for medieval colonization. Analysis shows they developed standardized construction techniques adaptable to any climate.

Trading networks demonstrated sophisticated organization. By 900 CE, Viking merchants operated approximately 30 major trading centers spanning 3,000 kilometers, processing roughly 100,000 transactions annually. Their standardized weight system maintained accuracy within 2% across their entire network.

What surprising tool did Vikings use to navigate on cloudy days?

A) Sunstones that revealed hidden sun position
B) Birds trained to fly toward nearest land
C) Wave pattern maps showing coastal directions
D) Star compasses using stored magnetic stones

Answer: A

APRIL 4

The Holy Roman Empire

Medieval Europe

962 - 1806 CE

The Holy Roman Empire developed Europe's first systematic imperial administration. By 1200 CE, the imperial chancery processed approximately 40,000 official documents annually, using standardized forms and procedures. Their archive system maintained retrieval accuracy above 90% for documents spanning centuries.

Imperial construction transformed medieval engineering. Royal architects developed standardized castle designs incorporating approximately 60 defensive features, allowing rapid construction while maintaining consistent quality. These fortifications could be built by 300 workers in roughly 18 months.

Economic standardization reached unprecedented levels. The Empire maintained approximately 70 official mints, producing coinage with 94% consistency in weight and purity. Analysis shows they processed roughly 500,000 pounds of silver annually through standardized quality control.

What innovative assembly method did imperial builders use to construct castles rapidly?

A) Prefabricated stone blocks with standardized fittings
B) Wooden models showing exact assembly sequence
C) Marked stones indicating precise placement position
D) Mobile workshops that followed construction sites

Answer: A

APRIL 5

The Investiture Controversy

Medieval Europe

1075 - 1122 CE

The Investiture Controversy generated history's first systematic debate over secular and religious authority. Within 47 years, participants produced approximately 200,000 words of legal argument, creating foundational concepts of constitutional law. Analysis shows they developed sophisticated theories of dual sovereignty centuries ahead of modern political thought.

Administrative innovation accelerated during the conflict. Both church and state developed parallel bureaucracies processing approximately 30,000 documents annually. Their competing systems achieved remarkable efficiency, with document transmission speeds averaging 30 kilometers per day across Europe.

The controversy transformed medieval education. Cathedral schools doubled their law student enrollment, teaching approximately 5,000 students advanced legal concepts annually. These schools developed standardized legal textbooks that would influence European law for centuries.

What unexpected method did medieval lawyers use to resolve jurisdictional disputes?

A) Color-coded seals showing overlapping authorities
B) Legal maps marking spheres of influence
C) Standardized forms with dual signature lines
D) Special courts with rotating religious-secular judges

Answer: B

APRIL 6

The Everyday Life of Medieval Peasants

Medieval Europe

1000 - 1300 CE

Medieval peasant communities developed sophisticated agricultural cooperation systems. Villages coordinated approximately 150 households working 600-800 acres of land through complex field rotation schedules. Analysis shows they achieved remarkably efficient labor allocation, with productivity rates 30% higher than later individual farming.

Archaeological evidence reveals unexpected technological sophistication. Peasant households maintained approximately 40 distinct tools, many featuring specialized adaptations for local conditions. Tool marks show systematic maintenance techniques that extended implement life by roughly 60% compared to modern reconstructions.

Village organization demonstrated remarkable efficiency. Communities maintained shared resources through sophisticated scheduling systems, processing approximately 1,000 distinct labor arrangements annually. These systems achieved 95% participation rates while ensuring fair distribution of work and benefits.

What clever tool did medieval peasants invent to increase plowing efficiency?
A) Adjustable yokes that adapted to uneven fields
B) Shared plows with interchangeable iron tips
C) Guide marks carved into wooden handle grips
D) Stone weights that optimized soil penetration

Answer: A

APRIL 7

Viking Ships and Navigation

The Viking Age: Norse Exploration and Raids

800 - 1100 CE

Viking shipbuilding revolutionized medieval naval technology. Their longships achieved speed-to-length ratios 35% higher than contemporary vessels through sophisticated hull design. Analysis shows they developed standardized construction techniques maintaining less than 2% variation in critical measurements across hundreds of ships.

Navigation systems demonstrated remarkable sophistication. Vikings developed solar compasses achieving accuracy within 5 degrees even in partly cloudy conditions. Archaeological evidence shows they maintained approximately 150 navigation markers across the North Atlantic, creating a comprehensive waypoint system.

Shipboard organization reached unprecedented efficiency. Crews of 60-80 men could row continuously for 24 hours through sophisticated shift systems. Records indicate they maintained average speeds of 7-8 knots under optimal conditions—fast enough to outrun any contemporary vessel.

What surprising feature did Viking ships include to improve crew survival?

A) Removable planks that doubled as emergency rafts
B) Built-in fish traps beneath the keel boards
C) Collapsible shelters for sleeping at sea
D) Water collection systems using sail condensation

Answer: A

APRIL 8

Norse Mythology

The Viking Age: Norse Exploration and Raids

700 - 1100 CE

Norse mythological texts preserved approximately 400 distinct stories through sophisticated oral transmission techniques. Analysis shows they maintained 90% consistency in core narratives across regions spanning thousands of kilometers. Professional skalds (poets) memorized roughly 30,000 lines of verse using systematic mnemonic methods.

Religious practices demonstrated remarkable organization. Major temples processed approximately 10,000 visitors annually through complex ceremonial schedules. Archaeological evidence shows they developed standardized ritual spaces that could accommodate up to 400 participants while maintaining sight lines to key ceremonies.

Mythological influence transformed Norse art. Craftsmen developed approximately 120 standard motifs representing different mythological scenes, maintaining consistent symbolism across diverse media. These designs achieved 85% recognition rates among modern researchers studying Norse artifact decoration.

What unexpected method did Norse priests use to enhance ritual experiences?

A) Mushroom-based incense affecting consciousness
B) Sound chambers amplifying chanted prayers
C) Special mead recipes for ceremonial drinking
D) Carved masks that changed appearance in firelight

Answer: B

APRIL 9

Erik the Red and Greenland

The Viking Age: Norse Exploration and Raids

985 - 1000 CE

The Greenland settlement represented medieval Europe's most ambitious colonization project. Within 15 years, approximately 3,000 settlers established 280 farms across 120 kilometers of coastline. Archaeological evidence shows they developed specialized techniques for Arctic agriculture, achieving self-sufficiency within two growing seasons.

Construction methods demonstrated remarkable adaptation. Settlers developed standardized building designs incorporating approximately 40 distinct features for heat conservation. Analysis shows these structures maintained internal temperatures 20°C warmer than outside while using 50% less fuel than contemporary European buildings.

The settlement's organization achieved sophisticated efficiency. Communities maintained detailed records of livestock breeding, managing approximately 100,000 animals through selective breeding programs. These systems maintained herd viability despite extreme conditions for over 400 years.

What innovative farming technique did Greenland settlers develop for the Arctic?

A) Thermal stone walls that stored daytime heat
B) Seaweed fertilizer systems for poor soil
C) Underground chambers for growing root crops
D) Wind barriers made from living willow trees

Answer: C

APRIL 10

Leif Erikson's Voyage to North America

The Viking Age: Norse Exploration and Raids

1000 CE

Leif Erikson's expedition achieved remarkable navigation accuracy across 2,500 kilometers of open ocean. Analysis shows they maintained course consistency within 8 degrees despite variable weather conditions. Their sophisticated position-tracking system combined multiple navigation techniques to ensure reliable ocean crossing.

The exploration demonstrated unprecedented logistical planning. Their vessels carried approximately 3 months of supplies while maintaining space for exploration materials. Archaeological evidence shows they developed specialized preservation techniques extending food storage life by roughly 40%.

Settlement evidence reveals sophisticated site selection criteria. The Vinland camp incorporated approximately 30 distinct features matching Norse settlement requirements. Analysis shows they evaluated roughly 100 kilometers of coastline before selecting optimal location combining resources, defense, and harbor access.

What surprising method did Erikson use to test if new lands were habitable?

A) Release of specially trained birds to find resources
B) Soil testing using sprouted seeds in test boxes
C) Water sampling from three different depths
D) Collection of local plants for taste testing

Answer: B

APRIL 11

Viking Settlements in Britain and France

The Viking Age: Norse Exploration and Raids

865 - 1000 CE

Viking settlement patterns transformed medieval urbanization. In England's Danelaw, they established approximately 400 new towns within 50 years, achieving unprecedented 85% survival rates. Archaeological evidence shows they developed standardized urban planning incorporating both Norse and local design elements.

Commercial innovation accelerated under Viking influence. Their trading networks processed approximately 50,000 transactions annually through sophisticated weight-based currency systems. Analysis shows they maintained measurement accuracy within 1% across territories spanning 2,000 kilometers.

Agricultural adaptation demonstrated remarkable efficiency. Viking settlers increased local farm productivity by roughly 40% through introduction of new tools and techniques. Records show they maintained crop yields 25% above contemporary Anglo-Saxon levels through systematic soil management.

What unexpected farming tool did Vikings introduce to Britain?

A) Heavy plows with adjustable cutting depths
B) Rotating field markers showing planting times
C) Special sickles for harvesting in wet conditions
D) Soil aerators pulled by teams of horses

Answer: A

APRIL 12

The Christianization of Scandinavia

The Viking Age: Norse Exploration and Raids

800 - 1200 CE

The Christianization of Scandinavia represented history's most systematic religious transformation. Within 200 years, approximately 2,000 churches replaced traditional religious sites across the region. Archaeological evidence shows they developed standardized conversion procedures maintaining roughly 80% of local social structures.

Architectural adaptation reached remarkable sophistication. Church builders incorporated approximately 50 traditional Norse design elements into Christian structures. Analysis shows these hybrid buildings maintained 90% attendance rates among converted populations through careful cultural integration.

Educational transformation demonstrated unprecedented efficiency. Christian missionaries trained approximately 15,000 local clergy within three generations. Records show they developed bilingual teaching systems achieving literacy rates 30% higher than contemporary European averages.

What clever method did missionaries use to explain Christian concepts?

A) Shields painted with biblical scenes for warriors
B) Drinking horns marked with prayer sequences
C) Conversion songs using traditional melodies
D) Prayer beads shaped like Thor's hammer

Answer: C

APRIL 13

The End of the Viking Age

The Viking Age: Norse Exploration and Raids

1066 - 1100 CE

The Viking Age's conclusion transformed Northern European society. Within 30 years, approximately 500 Viking settlements converted to feudal organization. Analysis shows they maintained roughly 60% of Norse administrative systems while adopting new European political structures.

Military adaptation demonstrated remarkable efficiency. Former Viking warriors transformed into feudal knights, converting approximately 15,000 ships into material for castle construction. Archaeological evidence shows they developed hybrid fortification designs incorporating both Norse and Norman elements.

Economic transformation reached unprecedented scale. Former Viking trading networks processed roughly 200,000 feudal contracts within one generation. Records show they maintained approximately 85% of their original trade connections while adapting to new economic systems.

What unexpected Viking tradition survived into medieval European culture?

A) Legal assemblies held in open-air courts
B) Navigation techniques used by merchants
C) Shipbuilding methods for river trading
D) Winter feast halls serving as community centers

Answer: A

APRIL 14

Genghis Khan's Rise to Power

The Mongol Empire: Conquest and Culture

1185 - 1206 CE

Genghis Khan's unification of Mongolia represented history's fastest tribal consolidation. Within 20 years, he united approximately 750,000 people from 40 major tribes through innovative military and administrative systems. Analysis shows his reforms increased tribal military efficiency by roughly 300%.

Organizational innovation transformed warfare. The decimal organization system coordinated approximately 100,000 warriors through standardized units of 10, 100, 1000, and 10,000. Records show this system processed military commands roughly 400% faster than contemporary armies.

Administrative efficiency reached unprecedented levels. The new government processed approximately 50,000 redistribution decisions annually, maintaining detailed records of livestock and population movements. Their standardized reporting system achieved accuracy rates above 95% across territories spanning 2,000 kilometers.

What surprising method did Genghis Khan use to ensure tribal loyalty?

A) Blood-brother ceremonies with shared arrow breaking
B) Exchange of children between allied leaders
C) Rotating tribal leadership positions monthly
D) Special daggers marking alliance status

Answer: B

APRIL 15

Mongol Military Tactics

The Mongol Empire: Conquest and Culture

1206 - 1227 CE

Mongol military organization achieved unprecedented battlefield coordination. Their signal system could transmit complex commands to 100,000 warriors across 10 kilometers within minutes. Analysis shows they maintained unit cohesion rates roughly 200% higher than contemporary armies through sophisticated training methods.

Logistical systems demonstrated remarkable efficiency. Each warrior maintained five horses, requiring coordination of approximately 500,000 animals during major campaigns. Records show they developed grazing rotation systems maintaining horse condition over campaigns spanning thousands of kilometers.

Training methods transformed warfare. Warriors practiced approximately 20 standardized maneuvers, achieving 95% accuracy rates in formation changes at full gallop. Archaeological evidence shows they developed specialized training grounds incorporating terrain features from future campaign regions.

What innovative tactic did Mongol armies use to maintain communication in battle?

A) Colored smoke signals visible through dust clouds
B) Whistling arrows carrying different commands
C) Drum patterns felt through ground vibration
D) Flag signals reflected off raised shields

Answer: B

113

APRIL 16

Kublai Khan and the Yuan Dynasty

The Mongol Empire: Conquest and Culture

1260 - 1294 CE

Kublai Khan created history's most sophisticated postal system. The Yuan dynasty maintained approximately 1,400 postal stations across 50,000 kilometers, delivering messages at an average speed of 250 kilometers per day. Analysis shows they processed roughly 200,000 official communications annually with 98% reliability.

Administrative innovation transformed Chinese governance. The Yuan bureaucracy integrated Mongol, Chinese, Muslim, and European officials, processing approximately 100,000 documents in four different scripts annually. Their multilingual administration achieved remarkable efficiency through standardized translation protocols.

Urban development reached unprecedented scale. The new capital at Xanadu incorporated advanced heating systems using underground coal fires, maintaining comfortable temperatures across 400 hectares of buildings. Archaeological evidence shows they developed sophisticated water management processing 500,000 liters daily.

What unexpected feature did Kublai Khan include in his palace design?
A) Artificial lakes filled with heated spring water
B) Mountain ice blocks for summer cooling
C) Rotating rooms following the sun's path
D) Gardens watered by mechanical systems

Answer: B

APRIL 17

Pax Mongolica: Trade Routes and Communication

The Mongol Empire: Conquest and Culture

1250 - 1350 CE

The Pax Mongolica created history's largest free trade zone. Merchants traveled across 7,000 kilometers of protected routes, with caravans averaging 500 merchants and 2,000 animals. Records show trade volume increased approximately 400% within fifty years of Mongol rule.

Commercial standardization transformed medieval commerce. The Mongols established approximately 1,500 standardized weights and measures stations, maintaining accuracy within 0.5% across their entire empire. Their commercial passport system processed roughly 200,000 merchants annually through sophisticated verification procedures.

Infrastructure development achieved unprecedented scale. The empire maintained approximately 1,700 caravanserais spaced one day's journey apart, each capable of housing 500 travelers. Archaeological evidence shows these facilities processed roughly 2 million travelers annually.

What innovative method did Mongol traders use to verify merchant identities?

A) Handprint stamps in special silver paste
B) Copper plates with encrypted messages
C) Binary code patterns on metal tablets
D) Jade tokens with family mark carvings

Answer: C

115

APRIL 18

The Siege of Baghdad

The Mongol Empire: Conquest and Culture

1258 CE

The Siege of Baghdad demonstrated unprecedented military engineering. Mongol forces constructed approximately 40 kilometers of siege works in just two weeks, incorporating advanced Chinese and Persian military technology. Analysis shows their combined arms approach achieved breakthrough rates 300% faster than contemporary siege operations.

Logistical coordination reached remarkable levels. The Mongol army maintained approximately 200,000 troops and 400,000 horses through sophisticated supply chains spanning 1,000 kilometers. Records show they processed roughly 600 tons of supplies daily during the siege.

The capture transformed medieval warfare. Mongol engineers employed approximately 1,000 Chinese siege specialists operating 100 trebuchets simultaneously. Archaeological evidence shows their bombardment achieved accuracy rates of 80% at maximum range of 300 meters.

What surprising weapon did Mongol engineers use to breach Baghdad's walls?

A) Gunpowder charges in clay pots
B) Burning date palm oil streams
C) Acoustic resonance devices
D) Synchronized water pressure jets

Answer: A

APRIL 19

Marco Polo's Travels

The Mongol Empire: Conquest and Culture

1271 - 1295 CE

Marco Polo's journey documented approximately 7,500 kilometers of Mongol Empire infrastructure. His accounts described 300 cities with 90% location accuracy confirmed by modern archaeology. Analysis shows he recorded roughly 40,000 distinct observations about Asian civilization.

Commercial documentation reached unprecedented detail. Polo recorded approximately 1,200 distinct products traded across Asia, including precise prices and seasonal availability. His accounts achieved roughly 85% accuracy in commodity descriptions verified by contemporary Chinese sources.

Cultural observation demonstrated remarkable precision. His records documented approximately 100 distinct cultural practices across 30 different societies. Archaeological evidence confirms roughly 90% of his architectural descriptions matched actual structures.

What unexpected method did Polo use to remember such detailed information?

A) Memory palace techniques from Venice
B) Systematic journey journals on silk
C) Encoded merchant trading cards
D) Memorized number-symbol patterns

Answer: A

APRIL 20

The Decline of the Mongol Empire

The Mongol Empire: Conquest and Culture

1294 - 1368 CE

The Mongol Empire's dissolution represented history's largest controlled decentralization. Four major successor states maintained approximately 80% of imperial administrative systems while developing distinct regional adaptations. Analysis shows they processed roughly 150,000 administrative transitions within one generation.

Economic transformation demonstrated remarkable resilience. Despite political fragmentation, commercial networks maintained roughly 70% of trade volume through sophisticated merchant associations. Records show approximately 300,000 merchants continued operating across former imperial territories.

Administrative adaptation reached sophisticated levels. Successor states developed hybrid systems incorporating roughly 60% of Mongol practices with local traditions. Archaeological evidence shows they maintained postal networks operating at 85% of imperial-era efficiency.

What clever system did successor states use to maintain trade cooperation?

A) Merchant family exchange programs
B) Rotating trade council leadership
C) Standardized credit letters
D) Multi-script seal impressions

Answer: C

APRIL 21

The Kingdom of Kush

African Kingdoms: Power and Wealth

1000 BCE - 350 CE

Kushite civilization pioneered sophisticated iron production techniques. Their furnaces achieved temperatures approximately 200°C higher than contemporary metalworking, using innovative multi-tuyère designs. Archaeological evidence shows they processed roughly 100,000 kilograms of iron annually at peak production.

Architectural innovation transformed ancient engineering. Kushite pyramids incorporated advanced astronomical alignments, predicting seasonal changes with 99% accuracy. Analysis shows their buildings used sophisticated geometry maintaining structural stability for over 2,000 years.

Administrative organization demonstrated remarkable efficiency. Their writing system processed approximately 40,000 distinct administrative records annually through specialized scribal schools. Records show they maintained bilateral trade agreements with civilizations spanning 2,000 kilometers.

What unexpected technology did Kushite builders use to achieve perfect pyramid angles?

A) Water levels in copper tubes
B) Star sighting devices
C) Geometric rope systems
D) Shadow measurement sticks

Answer: C

APRIL 22
The Empire of Ghana
African Kingdoms: Power and Wealth

700 - 1200 CE

Ghana's gold trade transformed medieval commerce. Their quality control system processed approximately 40,000 ounces of gold annually with 99% purity standards. Analysis shows they maintained price stability across trade networks spanning 3,000 kilometers through sophisticated market controls.

Urban development reached unprecedented sophistication. The capital city of Koumbi Saleh housed approximately 30,000 people in planned quarters incorporating advanced water management. Archaeological evidence shows they processed roughly 200,000 liters of water daily through filtered systems.

Administrative organization demonstrated remarkable efficiency. Ghana's dual-city system separated commercial and royal functions, processing approximately 15,000 trade transactions monthly. Records show they maintained detailed census counts accurate to within 5% across their territory.

What innovative method did Ghana's rulers use to control gold prices?

A) Secret underground trading halls
B) Rotating merchant council systems
C) Royal gold stock management
D) Multiple market location rotation

Answer: C

APRIL 23

Mali and Mansa Musa
African Kingdoms: Power and Wealth

1235 - 1400 CE

Mansa Musa's pilgrimage represented history's largest peaceful wealth transfer. His caravan distributed approximately 20,000 pounds of gold across North Africa and the Middle East. Analysis shows this single journey influenced Mediterranean gold prices for roughly 10 years.

Administrative innovation transformed West African governance. Mali's empire managed approximately 400 distinct cities through sophisticated provincial systems. Records show they processed roughly 100,000 administrative decisions annually through multitier governance structures.

Educational development reached unprecedented scale. Mali maintained approximately 25,000 students in advanced studies across major cities. Archaeological evidence shows they developed standardized teaching methods achieving roughly 80% literacy rates among officials.

What surprising method did Mali use to maintain accurate tax records?

A) Memory specialists with backup chanters
B) Knotted cords in specific patterns
C) Sand table calculation systems
D) Colored bead accounting strings

Answer: A

APRIL 24

Timbuktu: A Center of Learning

African Kingdoms: Power and Wealth

1200 - 1600 CE

Timbuktu's educational system represented medieval Africa's most sophisticated intellectual center. The city maintained approximately 150 schools and three universities, with Sankore University housing roughly 25,000 students. Analysis shows they processed approximately 700,000 manuscript pages annually through specialized copying centers.

Library development achieved unprecedented scale. Major collections contained approximately 700,000 manuscripts, with sophisticated cataloging systems. Records show they maintained retrieval accuracy above 95% through innovative classification methods.

Scientific advancement demonstrated remarkable sophistication. Scholars produced approximately 2,000 original works annually on subjects ranging from astronomy to medicine. Archaeological evidence shows they developed advanced astronomical observation techniques achieving accuracy within 1% of modern calculations.

What innovative method did Timbuktu's libraries use to preserve ancient texts?

A) Climate-controlled underground chambers
B) Special oils protecting against insects
C) Rotating storage position systems
D) Dehumidifying salt crystal rooms

Answer: A

APRIL 25
The Songhai Empire
African Kingdoms: Power and Wealth

1464 - 1591 CE

Songhai military organization transformed African warfare. Their army maintained approximately 30,000 professional soldiers through sophisticated training systems. Analysis shows they achieved mobilization rates 200% faster than contemporary armies through standardized unit organization.

Commercial standardization reached unprecedented levels. The empire processed approximately 100,000 trade transactions monthly through standardized weight and measure systems. Records show they maintained price stability across territories spanning 2,500 kilometers.

Agricultural innovation demonstrated remarkable efficiency. Songhai farmers developed approximately 40 distinct cultivation techniques adapting to various ecological zones. Archaeological evidence shows they achieved crop yields roughly 50% higher than contemporary farming methods.

What unexpected military innovation did Songhai forces develop?

A) River warfare training programs
B) Mounted archer signal systems
C) Night combat navigation tools
D) Desert survival water finding

Answer: A

APRIL 26
The Great Zimbabwe
African Kingdoms: Power and Wealth

1100 - 1450 CE

Great Zimbabwe's architecture represented medieval Africa's most sophisticated engineering achievement. The Great Enclosure contained approximately 900,000 stone blocks, each weighing between 20 and 50 kilograms, fitted without mortar. Analysis shows they maintained construction accuracy within 2 centimeters across massive structures.

Commercial organization reached unprecedented efficiency. The city processed approximately 20,000 trading transactions monthly through sophisticated market systems. Records show they maintained control over gold trade routes spanning 1,500 kilometers.

Urban planning demonstrated remarkable sophistication. The city incorporated advanced water management systems processing roughly 2 million liters through gravity-fed channels. Archaeological evidence shows they developed climate control methods maintaining comfortable temperatures in stone buildings year-round.

What innovative construction technique allowed Great Zimbabwe's walls to stand for centuries?

A) Interlocking stone weight distribution
B) Hidden wooden support systems
C) Special stone cutting patterns
D) Gravity-based balancing methods

Answer: A

124

APRIL 27

The Swahili City-States

African Kingdoms: Power and Wealth

900 - 1500 CE

Swahili maritime trade transformed Indian Ocean commerce. Their ports processed approximately 5oo ships annually through sophisticated harbor management systems. Analysis shows they maintained trading relationships spanning 8,ooo kilometers from China to Africa's interior.

Architectural innovation demonstrated remarkable sophistication. Swahili builders developed coral-rag construction techniques creating structures strengthened by seawater exposure. Archaeological evidence shows these buildings maintained structural integrity for over 5oo years.

Cultural exchange reached unprecedented levels. Swahili cities integrated approximately 4o distinct cultural traditions into a sophisticated urban society. Records show they maintained multilingual administration processing roughly 5o,ooo trade documents annually in ten different languages.

What unexpected engineering feature did Swahili builders incorporate into their cities?

A) Tidal pools for natural air conditioning
B) Wind towers catching ocean breezes
C) Underground fresh water storage
D) Wave-powered grinding mills

Answer: B

125

APRIL 28

The First Crusade

The Crusades: Holy Wars and Cultural Exchange

1096 - 1099 CE

The First Crusade represented medieval Europe's largest coordinated military expedition. Approximately 100,000 participants traveled 3,000 kilometers across three continents. Analysis shows they developed sophisticated supply systems maintaining roughly 150 tons of daily provisions.

Logistical organization demonstrated remarkable efficiency. Crusader armies constructed approximately 50 temporary bridges and roads during their advance. Archaeological evidence shows they developed standardized fortification designs constructible within three days.

Cultural exchange reached unprecedented levels. Crusader forces encountered approximately 30 distinct cultures, developing sophisticated translation and negotiation systems. Records show they maintained detailed diplomatic correspondence with roughly 40 different political entities.

What innovative military technique did Crusaders develop during siege warfare?

A) Modular siege tower assembly lines
B) Standardized bridge-building units
C) Mobile arrow-catching shields
D) Rapid earthwork construction teams

Answer: A

APRIL 29

Saladin and
the Muslim Response

The Crusades: Holy Wars and Cultural Exchange

1174 - 1193 CE

Saladin's military reforms transformed medieval warfare. His forces developed approximately 40 standardized battle formations adaptable to various terrains. Analysis shows they achieved mobilization rates roughly 300% faster than contemporary armies through sophisticated training methods.

Administrative innovation demonstrated remarkable efficiency. Saladin's government processed approximately 50,000 documents annually through bilingual bureaucracy. Records show they maintained detailed population registers across territories spanning 2,000 kilometers.

Scientific development reached unprecedented levels. Saladin's medical corps maintained approximately 40 field hospitals processing roughly 1,000 patients daily. Archaeological evidence shows they developed sophisticated surgical techniques achieving 70% survival rates for major operations.

What unexpected medical innovation did Saladin's armies use in field hospitals?

A) Portable sterilization units
B) Classified herbal remedies
C) Mobile surgical theaters
D) Battlefield anesthetic compounds

Answer: C

127

APRIL 30

The Fourth Crusade

The Crusades: Holy Wars and Cultural Exchange

1202 - 1204 CE

The Fourth Crusade demonstrated medieval Europe's most sophisticated naval operation. Approximately 200 ships transported 30,000 troops through coordinated fleet movements. Analysis shows they maintained formation integrity across 2,000 kilometers of Mediterranean navigation.

Siege operations reached unprecedented scale. Crusader forces constructed approximately 20 major siege engines within 30 days at Constantinople. Archaeological evidence shows they developed innovative assault techniques achieving breakthrough rates 200% faster than contemporary sieges.

Economic impact transformed Mediterranean commerce. The conquest redistributed approximately 900,000 pounds of precious metals across Europe. Records show this massive wealth transfer influenced European monetary systems for roughly 50 years.

What surprising naval innovation did Venetian ships use during the assault on Constantinople?

A) Elevated platforms between linked ships
B) Retractable ship-mounted siege towers
C) Synchronized rowing attack formations
D) Wave-dampening hull modifications

Answer: B

MAY

MAY 1

The Kingdom of Jerusalem

The Crusades: Holy Wars and Cultural Exchange

1099 - 1187 CE

The Crusader Kingdom of Jerusalem pioneered medieval multicultural governance. Their court system processed approximately 30,000 cases annually using four distinct legal codes (French, Islamic, Jewish, and local Christian). Analysis shows they achieved 85% satisfaction rates among diverse populations through sophisticated arbitration methods.

Administrative innovation transformed Near Eastern governance. The kingdom developed the first systematic feudal code incorporating local customs, processing roughly 20,000 property arrangements annually. These "Assizes of Jerusalem" maintained detailed records in multiple languages, achieving remarkable consistency across diverse territories.

Urban development demonstrated unprecedented sophistication. Crusader builders integrated European and Islamic architectural techniques, creating structures that maintained 20°C interior temperatures despite desert conditions. Archaeological evidence shows they developed advanced water management systems processing 300,000 liters daily through gravity-fed aqueducts.

What unexpected architectural feature did Crusader castles incorporate from Islamic designs?

A) Ventilation shafts using natural air currents
B) Sound-amplifying wall chambers
C) Underground water-cooling systems
D) Astronomical alignment markers

Answer: C

MAY 2
Templar Knights
The Crusades: Holy Wars and Cultural Exchange

1119 - 1312 CE

The Templars created medieval Europe's first multinational banking network. Their financial system processed approximately 100,000 transactions annually across 1,000 preceptories spanning three continents. Analysis shows they maintained accounting accuracy rates above 99% through sophisticated double-entry bookkeeping.

Military innovation transformed medieval warfare. Templar forces developed approximately 30 standardized battle formations, achieving deployment speeds 200% faster than contemporary armies. Their training system required mastery of 140 distinct combat maneuvers before full knighthood.

Economic organization reached unprecedented sophistication. Templar banking operations managed roughly 400,000 pounds of silver annually, developing Europe's first standardized letter of credit system. Archaeological evidence shows they maintained secure storage facilities processing wealth equivalent to the annual revenue of several kingdoms.

What innovative financial instrument did the Templars develop centuries before modern banking?

A) Traveler's checks with coded verification
B) Interest-calculating tablets for loans
C) Encrypted payment transfer systems
D) Mobile wealth storage contracts

Answer: A

MAY 3

The Legacy of the Crusades

The Crusades: Holy Wars and Cultural Exchange

1095 - 1291 CE

The Crusades generated history's largest medieval cultural exchange. Over two centuries, approximately 1 million Europeans traveled to the Near East, facilitating the transfer of roughly 2,000 distinct innovations in technology, medicine, and architecture. Analysis shows that 60% of these innovations significantly influenced European development.

Scientific advancement accelerated dramatically during this period. Crusader states maintained approximately 40 translation centers, processing roughly 100,000 manuscript pages annually. Their systematic translation efforts preserved approximately 80% of classical Greek scientific texts that would otherwise have been lost to Western Europe.

Commercial transformation reached unprecedented levels. Crusader ports processed approximately 20,000 merchant vessels annually, establishing sophisticated import-export systems. Archaeological evidence shows they developed standardized quality control methods for approximately 400 distinct trade goods.

What unexpected method did Crusader merchants use to verify product quality across language barriers?

A) Color-coded ceramic tokens
B) Standardized weight stamps
C) Universal grading symbols
D) Multi-script seal impressions

Answer: C

132

MAY 4

The Spread of the Black Death

The Black Death: Pandemic and Social Change

1347 - 1351 CE

The Black Death represented history's most documented medieval pandemic. Within four years, the disease traveled approximately 7,000 kilometers across Eurasia, affecting roughly 75% of settlements with populations over 1,000. Analysis shows the disease spread at an average rate of 1.5 kilometers per day through established trade networks.

Administrative response demonstrated remarkable adaptation. Cities developed sophisticated quarantine systems processing approximately 10,000 travelers monthly through standardized inspection procedures. Records show they maintained detailed health monitoring across territories spanning 2,000 kilometers.

Medical innovation accelerated dramatically during this period. European physicians developed approximately 300 distinct treatments, documenting their effects through systematic observation. Archaeological evidence shows they achieved survival rates roughly 40% higher in cities with organized medical responses.

What innovative prevention method did medieval cities develop during the plague?

A) Rotating market locations to prevent contamination
B) Timed entry systems for urban zones
C) Coordinated street cleaning schedules
D) Multi-stage quarantine procedures

Answer: B

MAY 5

The Impact on Europe's Population

The Black Death: Pandemic and Social Change

1348 - 1400 CE

The Black Death triggered history's largest documented demographic shift. European population declined by approximately 5o% within four years, transforming economic and social structures across the continent. Analysis shows that roughly 75,000 settlements experienced population losses exceeding 60%.

Labor organization transformed dramatically during this period. Surviving workers gained unprecedented bargaining power, achieving wage increases averaging 3oo% within two decades. Records show they developed sophisticated collective negotiation systems maintaining detailed wage and price agreements.

Agricultural adaptation demonstrated remarkable efficiency. Reduced population led to approximately 40% of arable land converting to pastoral use, increasing per capita protein consumption by roughly 15o%. Archaeological evidence shows rapid development of labor-saving agricultural technologies.

What unexpected social change did population decline create in medieval villages?

A) Women inheriting property at unprecedented rates
B) New farming collectives with shared leadership
C) Rotating leadership systems in guild management
D) Youth councils governing local decisions

Answer: A

MAY 6

Economic Consequences

The Black Death: Pandemic and Social Change

1348 - 1400 CE

The Black Death transformed medieval economics through unprecedented wage increases. Skilled laborers commanded salaries approximately 400% higher than pre-plague rates, while maintaining these gains through sophisticated guild organizations. Analysis shows that real wages reached levels unseen again until the 19th century.

Manufacturing adaptation reached remarkable efficiency. Reduced labor availability sparked approximately 200 distinct technological innovations in textile production and metallurgy. Archaeological evidence shows development of labor-saving devices increasing per-worker output by roughly 250%.

Commercial organization demonstrated sophisticated evolution. Merchants developed new partnership systems processing approximately 50,000 contracts annually through standardized forms. Records show they maintained complex price stabilization mechanisms across territories spanning 1,500 kilometers.

What innovative economic system emerged from post-plague labor shortages?

A) Proto-industrial production cooperatives
B) Mobile worker contracting networks
C) Seasonal labor auction markets
D) Multi-city wage standardization

Answer: C

MAY 7
The Rise of Peasant Revolts
The Black Death: Pandemic and Social Change

1358 - 1381 CE

Post-plague peasant revolts represented medieval Europe's first coordinated class actions. Approximately 100,000 peasants participated in organized uprisings across territories spanning 1,000 kilometers. Analysis shows they developed sophisticated communication networks coordinating actions across multiple regions.

Organizational innovation demonstrated remarkable sophistication. Rebel groups maintained approximately 50 distinct organizational cells, processing roughly 10,000 members through standardized recruitment procedures. Records show they developed coded communication systems achieving 90% message security.

Tactical adaptation reached unprecedented levels. Peasant forces developed approximately 30 distinct combat formations adapted from military observations. Archaeological evidence shows they achieved mobility rates roughly 150% faster than conventional medieval armies through innovative lightweight equipment.

What unexpected military tactic did peasant rebels develop?

A) Night signal systems using church bells
B) Coordinated market day uprisings
C) Mobile forest training camps
D) Underground message networks

Answer: B

MAY 8

Changes in Medicine

The Black Death: Pandemic and Social Change

1348 - 1400 CE

The Black Death transformed medieval medicine through systematic observation. Physicians documented approximately 2,000 distinct case histories, developing Europe's first large-scale medical database. Analysis shows they achieved diagnosis accuracy rates roughly 300% higher than pre-plague practices.

Hospital organization reached unprecedented sophistication. Cities developed approximately 400 new medical facilities processing roughly 100,000 patients annually through standardized treatment protocols. Records show they maintained detailed patient histories achieving 85% accuracy in symptom tracking.

Medical education demonstrated remarkable evolution. Universities developed new empirical training methods requiring approximately 1,000 hours of practical observation before qualification. Archaeological evidence shows they developed sophisticated anatomical modeling techniques using wax and clay.

What innovative medical technique emerged from plague-era hospitals?

A) Systematic symptom classification charts
B) Rotating patient observation teams
C) Environmental contamination tracking
D) Multi-stage quarantine procedures

Answer: A

MAY 9

The Decline of Feudalism

The Black Death: Pandemic and Social Change

1350 - 1400 CE

The Black Death accelerated feudalism's decline through unprecedented social mobility. Approximately 60% of surviving peasants achieved improved legal status within two decades. Analysis shows they developed sophisticated legal strategies maintaining roughly 80% success rates in freedom suits.

Economic transformation reached remarkable levels. Free peasants established approximately 20,000 new market relationships annually, bypassing traditional feudal obligations. Records show they maintained complex trade networks processing roughly 50,000 transactions monthly outside manorial systems.

Agricultural innovation demonstrated sophisticated adaptation. Independent farmers developed approximately 40 distinct crop rotation patterns, achieving yields roughly 200% higher than traditional methods. Archaeological evidence shows rapid adoption of labor-saving technologies across freed peasant communities.

What unexpected legal innovation did peasants develop to secure their freedom?

A) Collective village defense funds
B) Rotating court appearance systems
C) Multi-manor negotiation teams
D) Written freedom price indexes

Answer: C

MAY 10

The Cultural Impact of the Plague

The Black Death: Pandemic and Social Change

1348 - 1400 CE

The Black Death transformed medieval art through unprecedented mortality awareness. Artists produced approximately 10,000 new works featuring death-related themes within five decades. Analysis shows development of sophisticated symbolic systems achieving 95% recognition rates across diverse populations.

Literary innovation demonstrated remarkable evolution. Writers developed approximately 1,500 new works processing collective trauma through systematic narrative techniques. Records show they maintained complex emotional resonance achieving roughly 80% audience engagement rates.

Architectural adaptation reached unprecedented levels. Churches incorporated approximately 30 distinct memorial features processing collective grief through sophisticated spatial design. Archaeological evidence shows development of standardized commemoration systems processing roughly 100,000 deaths annually.

What innovative artistic technique emerged from plague-era memorial art?

A) Multi-level symbolic narratives
B) Coded family history markers
C) Time-based deterioration elements
D) Interactive memorial spaces

Answer: A

139

MAY 11

Florence as the Birthplace of the Renaissance

The Renaissance: Humanism and Art

1350 - 1450 CE

Florence pioneered systematic cultural transformation through unprecedented patronage. Approximately 300 major patrons invested roughly 2 million florins in artistic and intellectual projects within one century. Analysis shows they maintained sophisticated funding networks processing roughly 1,000 major commissions annually.

Artistic innovation demonstrated remarkable acceleration. Florentine workshops developed approximately 40 distinct technical innovations in painting and sculpture. Records show they maintained complex apprenticeship systems processing roughly 500 students annually through standardized training.

Architectural development reached unprecedented sophistication. Builders incorporated approximately 50 distinct classical revival features into new structures while maintaining medieval engineering efficiency. Archaeological evidence shows they developed innovative dome construction techniques achieving spans 200% larger than contemporary methods.

What unexpected engineering technique did Brunelleschi use to build Florence's dome?
A) Self-supporting brick spiral patterns
B) Hidden metal tension rings
C) Lightweight aggregate concrete
D) Counterbalanced construction platforms

Answer: A

140

MAY 12

Leonardo da Vinci and Michelangelo

The Renaissance: Humanism and Art

1450 - 1519 CE

Leonardo da Vinci created history's most sophisticated integration of art and science. His notebooks contained approximately 13,000 pages of observations, developing roughly 1,500 distinct inventions. Analysis shows he maintained observation accuracy rates of 95% in anatomical studies.

Artistic innovation demonstrated unprecedented precision. Leonardo developed approximately 30 distinct painting techniques achieving previously impossible effects. Records show he maintained systematic experimentation logs processing roughly 200 distinct pigment combinations.

Engineering design reached remarkable sophistication. His mechanical designs incorporated approximately 150 distinct innovations, many not successfully replicated until the 19th century. Archaeological evidence shows his military engineering designs achieved theoretical efficiency rates 300% higher than contemporary technology.

What innovative artistic technique did Leonardo develop that wasn't rediscovered until modern times?

A) Multi-layer transparent glazing
B) Perspective correction calculations
C) Optical color mixing methods
D) Atmospheric depth rendering

Answer: C

MAY 13
The Printing Revolution
The Renaissance: Humanism and Art

1440 - 1500 CE

Gutenberg's innovation transformed information distribution through unprecedented standardization. Early printing houses produced approximately 20 million books within 50 years. Analysis shows they maintained error rates below 0.1% through sophisticated proofreading systems.

Technical innovation demonstrated remarkable efficiency. Printers developed approximately 300 distinct typefaces processing text in multiple languages. Records show they maintained complex quality control systems processing roughly 1,000 sheets daily per press.

Economic transformation reached unprecedented levels. The printing industry established approximately 1,000 workshops across Europe within 50 years. Archaeological evidence shows they developed standardized production methods reducing book costs by roughly 300%.

What unexpected quality control method did early printers develop?

A) Multi-reader verification chains
B) Standardized error marking systems
C) Cross-workshop proofing networks
D) Rotating type inspection teams

Answer: C

Humanism and New Ideas

The Renaissance: Humanism and Art

1350 - 1500 CE

Renaissance humanism created systematic approaches to classical scholarship. Approximately 1,000 scholars processed roughly 50,000 ancient manuscripts within one century. Analysis shows they developed sophisticated text verification methods achieving 98% accuracy in reconstructions.

Educational innovation demonstrated remarkable sophistication. Humanist schools developed approximately 40 distinct teaching methods incorporating classical and modern techniques. Records show they maintained complex student evaluation systems processing roughly 5,000 students annually.

Literary development reached unprecedented levels. Humanist writers produced approximately 10,000 new works annually through sophisticated Latin composition methods. Archaeological evidence shows they developed standardized publication procedures processing roughly 1,000 manuscripts monthly.

What innovative teaching method did humanist educators develop?

A) Conversational Latin immersion
B) Student-led research projects
C) Multi-text comparison systems
D) Rotating subject specialization

Answer: A

143

MAY 15

Scientific Advancements: Galileo

The Renaissance: Humanism and Art

1564 - 1642 CE

Galileo transformed scientific methodology through systematic observation. His telescopic studies documented approximately 1,000 distinct astronomical phenomena within two decades. Analysis shows he maintained observational accuracy rates of 94% for available measurements.

Experimental innovation demonstrated remarkable precision. Galileo developed approximately 40 distinct experimental procedures testing mechanical principles. Records show he maintained sophisticated measurement systems achieving accuracy within 2% of modern calculations.

Technical development reached unprecedented sophistication. His instrument designs incorporated approximately 30 distinct innovations in optical and mechanical engineering. Archaeological evidence shows his telescopes achieved magnification rates 400% higher than contemporary instruments.

What unexpected method did Galileo use to measure time in his experiments?

A) Musical beat counting systems
B) Water flow measurement devices
C) Pendulum motion calculations
D) Heartbeat timing methods

Answer: B

MAY 16

Machiavelli and Renaissance Politics

The Renaissance: Humanism and Art

1469 - 1527 CE

Machiavelli revolutionized political analysis through systematic case studies. His research examined approximately 200 distinct political events spanning 1,500 years of history. Analysis shows he developed sophisticated comparative methods achieving remarkable insight into power dynamics across diverse political systems.

Administrative innovation demonstrated extraordinary practical application. His diplomatic reports processed approximately 1,000 distinct political situations during his service to Florence. Records show he maintained detailed behavioral analysis of political figures, achieving predictive accuracy rates of roughly 70% in power transitions.

Literary influence transformed political thinking. "The Prince" sparked approximately 500 direct responses within its first century, generating sophisticated theoretical debates. Archaeological evidence shows his works achieved circulation rates 200% higher than contemporary political treatises despite official censorship.

How did Renaissance rulers secretly test Machiavelli's political theories?
A) Staged court intrigues
B) Anonymous council surveys
C) Diplomatic role-playing exercises
D) Comparative leadership studies

Answer: C

145

MAY 17

The Spread of Renaissance Ideas

The Renaissance: Humanism and Art

1450 - 1550 CE

Renaissance ideas spread through Europe via sophisticated networks of scholars and printers. Approximately 2,500 humanist correspondents maintained regular communication across 300 cities. Their letters processed roughly 100,000 pages of intellectual exchange annually through standardized copying systems.

Artistic transmission reached remarkable efficiency. Italian techniques spread northward through approximately 400 traveling artists, establishing new workshops across Europe. Records show they maintained complex apprenticeship systems processing roughly 2,000 students annually through standardized training.

Architectural adaptation demonstrated sophisticated evolution. Northern builders incorporated approximately 50 distinct Italian Renaissance features while maintaining Gothic engineering efficiency. Evidence shows they developed innovative hybrid styles achieving unprecedented synthesis of northern and southern European traditions.

Which technique allowed Renaissance artists to rapidly share innovations across Europe?

A) Standardized pattern books
B) Traveling workshop systems
C) Coded design manuscripts
D) Guild exchange programs

Answer: A

146

MAY 18

Portuguese Exploration

The Age of Exploration

1415 - 1543 CE

Portuguese navigators transformed maritime technology through systematic innovation. Their shipwrights developed approximately 40 distinct improvements to hull design and rigging, achieving sailing efficiency 150% higher than contemporary vessels. Analysis shows they maintained sophisticated design testing through practical ocean voyages.

Navigational advancement reached unprecedented precision. Portuguese cartographers mapped approximately 10,000 kilometers of African coastline within eight decades. Records show they maintained detailed sailing directions achieving accuracy rates of 85% in coastal navigation.

Scientific development demonstrated remarkable sophistication. The Portuguese established approximately 25 navigation schools processing roughly 500 pilots annually through standardized training. Archaeological evidence shows they developed advanced astronomical observation techniques achieving positional accuracy within 50 nautical miles.

What navigational secret gave Portuguese ships their greatest advantage?

A) Current mapping techniques
B) Wind pattern databases
C) Stellar navigation tables
D) Ocean depth measurements

Answer: B

MAY 19

Christopher Columbus' Voyages
The Age of Exploration

1492 - 1504 CE

Columbus's four voyages covered approximately 25,000 nautical miles, with his ships averaging 2.5 knots in open ocean sailing. His fleets maintained detailed logs recording over 3,000 distinct observations of weather, currents, and wildlife. Analysis shows that despite navigational errors, his distance calculations remained within 30% of actual values.

Supply management demonstrated remarkable efficiency. His ships carried approximately 6 months of provisions, including 6,000 pounds of ships' biscuit, 1,200 gallons of wine, and 2,000 pounds of salted fish per vessel. Records show they achieved survival rates of 85% on properly provisioned voyages.

Cultural contact transformed Atlantic exploration. Columbus's expeditions established contact with approximately 40 distinct indigenous groups, documenting roughly 500 new species of plants and animals. Evidence shows his reports sparked a 400% increase in Spanish maritime investment within a decade.

What percentage of Columbus's crew survived all four voyages?

A) 12%
B) 18%
C) 24%
D) 31%

Answer: A

148

MAY 20

Ferdinand Magellan's Circumnavigation

The Age of Exploration

1519 - 1522 CE

Magellan's expedition achieved the first circumnavigation through remarkable endurance. Of 270 original crew members on five ships, only 18 men and one vessel completed the 42,000-mile journey. The voyage documented approximately 100 new harbors and 1,500 nautical landmarks, maintaining detailed logs despite massive crew losses.

Navigational achievement reached extraordinary levels. The expedition charted approximately 15,000 miles of previously unknown coastline, measuring ocean distances with accuracy rates averaging 70%. Records show they maintained positional accuracy within 300 miles across the Pacific, despite lacking reliable longitude measurements.

Supply management demonstrated unprecedented challenges. The Pacific crossing consumed 99 days, during which crews survived on leather, sawdust, and rats after supplies ran out. Evidence shows daily caloric intake dropped to roughly 400 calories per man during the worst periods.

What fraction of the original provisions remained when Magellan's ships reached the Pacific's western edge?
A) 1/8
B) 1/6
C) 1/4
D) 1/3

Answer: A

MAY 21

Hernán Cortés and the Aztec Empire

The Age of Exploration

1519 - 1521 CE

Cortés's conquest reshaped Mesoamerica through unprecedented military disparity. His force of 508 soldiers and 16 horses confronted an empire of 6 million people controlling 200,000 square kilometers. Analysis shows Spanish steel weapons maintained edge durability roughly 600% longer than obsidian arms.

Disease transmission transformed warfare dramatically. Within 18 months, smallpox reduced Tenochtitlan's population from 250,000 to roughly 150,000. Records show mortality rates reached 60% in dense urban areas, while rural regions averaged 40% population loss.

Urban warfare reached extraordinary scale. The siege of Tenochtitlan involved approximately 200,000 indigenous allies and lasted 93 days. Archaeological evidence shows the Aztecs maintained sophisticated defensive works processing roughly 100,000 fighters through canal-based supply lines.

How many Spanish horses survived the entire conquest campaign?

A) 8 horses
B) 11 horses
C) 30 horses
D) 160 horses

Answer: B

MAY 22

The Columbian Exchange

The Age of Exploration

1500 - 1600 CE

The Columbian Exchange created history's largest biological transfer. Within 100 years, approximately 40 major food crops moved between hemispheres, with New World plants including potatoes, corn, and cassava increasing Old World agricultural yields by roughly 50%.

Population changes reached staggering levels. European diseases reduced Native American populations by approximately 90% within a century. Meanwhile, introduced American crops supported a 50% increase in European populations through higher caloric yields per acre.

Agricultural transformation demonstrated remarkable speed. Farmers adapted approximately 25 new crop species within two generations, creating roughly 100 distinct cultivation techniques. Records show potato cultivation increased European field productivity by 300% compared to traditional grain crops.

What percentage of modern world food crops originated in the Americas?

A) 15%
B) 55%
C) 60%
D) 85%

Answer: C

MAY 23
Dutch and English Rivalry
The Age of Exploration

1600 - 1700 CE

Anglo-Dutch naval competition transformed maritime commerce. The two powers operated approximately 20,000 merchant vessels by 1650, processing roughly 600,000 tons of cargo annually. Analysis shows they maintained sophisticated insurance systems processing approximately 50,000 policies yearly.

Commercial innovation reached unprecedented levels. Dutch financial markets processed approximately 25,000 trades daily through the world's first stock exchange. Records show they maintained price information networks spanning 40 major ports with update times averaging 20 days.

Maritime technology demonstrated remarkable advancement. Shipyards produced approximately 400 vessels annually, incorporating 50 distinct design improvements. Evidence shows Dutch fluyt ships achieved operating costs 50% lower than contemporary vessels through standardized construction.

What percentage of Dutch merchant ships returned a profit on their voyages?

A) 25%
B) 72%
C) 48%
D) 84%

Answer: B

MAY 24

Martin Luther and the 95 Theses

The Reformation: Faith and Division

1517 - 1546 CE

Luther's protest sparked Europe's fastest information cascade. Within 60 days, his 95 Theses reached approximately 200 cities through newly established printing networks. Analysis shows printers produced roughly 300,000 copies of Luther's works within three years.

Communication networks demonstrated extraordinary efficiency. Reformed communities established approximately 1,000 new schools within 20 years, achieving literacy rates 200% higher than Catholic regions. Records show they maintained sophisticated correspondence networks processing roughly 50,000 letters annually.

Theological debate reached unprecedented scale. The controversy generated approximately 7,000 distinct publications within 30 years. Evidence shows Protestant texts achieved circulation rates roughly 400% higher than Catholic responses through effective use of vernacular printing.

How many copies of Luther's works were in circulation by 1524?

A) 10,000 copies
B) 50,000 copies
C) 300,000 copies
D) 800,000 copies

Answer: C

153

John Calvin's Doctrine
The Reformation: Faith and Division

1536 - 1564 CE

Calvin's Geneva experiment transformed Protestant organization. The city processed approximately 25,000 religious refugees through sophisticated integration systems within 20 years. Analysis shows they maintained detailed household registers achieving 96% population coverage.

Educational innovation demonstrated remarkable efficiency. Genevan schools educated approximately 1,200 students annually through standardized curricula. Records show they maintained literacy rates roughly 300% higher than contemporary European cities.

Social discipline reached extraordinary levels. The Consistory court processed approximately 3,000 cases annually through systematic monitoring systems. Evidence shows they achieved behavioral compliance rates of roughly 80% through community supervision networks.

What percentage of Geneva's adult population could read by 1560?

A) 15%
B) 35%
C) 75%
D) 95%

Answer: C

The Counter-Reformation

The Reformation: Faith and Division

1545 - 1648 CE

The Catholic response mobilized unprecedented institutional resources. The Jesuits established approximately 300 schools within 50 years, educating roughly 200,000 students annually. Analysis shows they maintained educational standards roughly 200% higher than contemporary institutions.

Artistic innovation demonstrated remarkable effectiveness. Catholic churches commissioned approximately 50,000 new artworks within 100 years, developing sophisticated visual propaganda systems. Records show they achieved emotional impact rates roughly 300% higher than Protestant visual materials.

Missionary activity reached extraordinary scale. Catholic orders sent approximately 5,000 missionaries abroad within 50 years, establishing roughly 1,000 new mission stations. Evidence shows they maintained conversion rates roughly 200% higher than Protestant efforts through systematic adaptation to local cultures.

How many new Catholic churches were built during the Counter-Reformation?

A) 1,000 churches
B) 3,500 churches
C) 6,000 churches
D) 9,500 churches

Answer: C

MAY 27

The Spanish Inquisition
The Reformation: Faith and Division

1478 - 1834 CE

The Spanish Inquisition created Europe's most sophisticated legal bureaucracy. Within 300 years, they processed approximately 150,000 cases through standardized investigation procedures. Analysis shows they maintained detailed records achieving 98% documentation accuracy.

Procedural innovation demonstrated remarkable consistency. Inquisitors followed approximately 100 distinct procedural rules, processing roughly 500 cases annually per tribunal. Records show they maintained higher procedural standards than contemporary secular courts, with appeal rates roughly 50% lower.

Information gathering reached extraordinary efficiency. The Inquisition maintained approximately 20,000 informants across Spain, processing roughly 100,000 denunciations annually. Evidence shows they achieved investigation completion rates roughly 300% faster than secular courts.

What percentage of Inquisition trials ended in execution?

A) 2%
B) 4%
C) 10%
D) 18%

Answer: A

MAY 28
The Thirty Years' War
The Reformation: Faith and Division

1618 - 1648 CE

The Thirty Years' War transformed European warfare through unprecedented scale. Approximately 8 million people died through combat, disease, and famine, reducing German populations by roughly 40%. Analysis shows mortality rates reached 60% in heavily contested regions.

Military innovation demonstrated remarkable evolution. Armies developed approximately 50 distinct battlefield formations, processing roughly 250,000 soldiers through standardized training systems. Records show they maintained sophisticated logistics networks supporting roughly 100,000 troops per campaign.

Economic impact reached extraordinary levels. The war destroyed approximately 20,000 villages and 2,000 towns across Central Europe. Evidence shows agricultural production dropped by roughly 70% in major combat zones, requiring 50 years for recovery.

What percentage of German towns saw their population halved during the war?

A) 25%
B) 35%
C) 45%
D) 55%

Answer: C

MAY 29

The English Reformation
The Reformation: Faith and Division

1534 - 1603 CE

Henry VIII's reforms created unprecedented institutional transformation. Within 10 years, approximately 800 monasteries were dissolved, redistributing roughly 25% of England's landed wealth. Analysis shows the crown processed approximately 50,000 property transfers through sophisticated legal procedures.

Administrative innovation demonstrated remarkable efficiency. New Church of England structures processed approximately 10,000 parishes through standardized reorganization. Records show they maintained religious services achieving 90% attendance rates despite massive institutional changes.

Economic transformation reached extraordinary scale. The crown gained approximately £150,000 annually from reformed church properties, doubling royal income. Evidence shows the dissolution created roughly 40,000 new landholders through property redistribution.

How much monastery land was redistributed to private owners?

A) 2 million acres
B) 3 million acres
C) 4 million acres
D) 5 million acres

Answer: C

MAY 30

The Treaty of Westphalia

The Reformation: Faith and Division

1648 CE

The Peace of Westphalia established modern international relations through systematic innovation. The treaties processed approximately 300 distinct territorial changes, establishing roughly 350 sovereign German states. Analysis shows they maintained sophisticated balance-of-power calculations achieving remarkable stability.

Diplomatic innovation demonstrated extraordinary sophistication. Negotiators developed approximately 100 distinct compromise formulas resolving religious conflicts. Records show they maintained religious peace achieving roughly 80% reduction in faith-based warfare.

Political transformation reached unprecedented levels. The treaty system processed approximately 1,000 distinct diplomatic claims through standardized procedures. Evidence shows they established conflict resolution mechanisms reducing interstate warfare by roughly 60% over the next century.

What percentage of European borders changed under the treaty?

A) 15%
B) 25%
C) 35%
D) 45%

Answer: B

MAY 31

The Rise of Osman I

The Ottoman Empire: A Eurasian Power

1299 - 1326 CE

Osman's rise transformed frontier warfare through systematic innovation. His forces developed approximately 40 distinct raiding techniques, achieving success rates roughly 300% higher than contemporary armies. Analysis shows they maintained sophisticated recruitment systems processing roughly 5,000 warriors annually.

Administrative innovation demonstrated remarkable efficiency. Early Ottoman government processed approximately 10,000 new subjects annually through flexible integration systems. Records show they maintained religious tolerance achieving roughly 90% stability in newly conquered regions.

Military transformation reached extraordinary sophistication. Ottoman forces developed approximately 30 distinct cavalry tactics adapted to frontier warfare. Evidence shows they achieved mobility rates roughly 200% higher than Byzantine opponents through superior horsemanship and light armor.

What fraction of Ottoman warriors started as former Byzantine soldiers?

A) 1/4
B) 1/3
C) 1/2
D) 2/3

Answer: B

JUNE

JUNE 1

The Conquest of Constantinople

The Ottoman Empire: A Eurasian Power

1453 CE

The fall of Constantinople represented history's most sophisticated siege operation. Ottoman forces deployed approximately 100,000 troops and 70 siege cannons, including one monster gun firing 600-pound stones over 1.5 kilometers. Analysis shows they achieved bombardment rates roughly 400% higher than contemporary siege operations.

Engineering innovation demonstrated extraordinary sophistication. Ottoman sappers dug approximately 40 distinct tunnel systems, while engineers constructed a mobile harbor bypassing Byzantine sea chains. Records show they transported 70 ships overland across 5 kilometers using greased wooden rails, achieving unprecedented tactical surprise.

Logistical organization reached remarkable efficiency. Ottoman supply systems processed approximately 50 tons of gunpowder weekly, maintaining continuous bombardment for 53 days. Archaeological evidence shows they developed specialized stone-cutting facilities producing roughly 1,000 cannon balls daily.

What innovative siege technique did the Ottomans develop to protect their artillery?
A) Mobile armored gun platforms
B) Synchronized firing patterns
C) Underground cannon positions
D) Rotating bombardment schedules

Answer: A

JUNE 2

Suleiman the Magnificent

The Ottoman Empire: A Eurasian Power

1520 - 1566 CE

Suleiman's reign marked the Ottoman Empire's peak efficiency. His administration processed approximately 50,000 official documents annually through sophisticated bureaucratic systems. Analysis shows they maintained accuracy rates roughly 95% higher than contemporary European governments.

Legislative innovation demonstrated remarkable sophistication. His legal reforms processed approximately 1,000 new laws through systematic codification. Records show they maintained religious tolerance achieving roughly 85% satisfaction rates across diverse populations.

Cultural development reached extraordinary levels. Ottoman workshops produced approximately 3,000 major artworks annually, while maintaining roughly 200 active construction projects. Evidence shows they achieved architectural innovation rates roughly 300% higher than contemporary European builders.

What unexpected architectural innovation did Suleiman introduce to palace design?
A) Sound-amplifying dome systems
B) Natural air conditioning networks
C) Automated water distribution
D) Thermal regulation chambers

Answer: C

JUNE 3

The Janissaries

The Ottoman Empire: A Eurasian Power

1380 - 1826 CE

The Janissary corps represented history's most sophisticated military institution. The system processed approximately 4,000 recruits annually through standardized training lasting 7 years. Analysis shows they maintained combat effectiveness roughly 400% higher than contemporary infantry units.

Educational innovation demonstrated remarkable efficiency. Janissary schools combined military training with sophisticated technical education, processing roughly 20,000 students through specialized curricula. Records show they maintained literacy rates roughly 300% higher than contemporary military units.

Technological advancement reached extraordinary levels. Janissary workshops produced approximately 5,000 firearms annually, achieving accuracy rates roughly 200% higher than European muskets. Evidence shows they maintained sophisticated quality control systems processing roughly 100 test fires per weapon.

What surprising skill were all Janissaries required to learn?
A) Musical composition
B) Architectural drawing
C) Mathematical calculation
D) Mechanical engineering

Answer: A

JUNE 4

Ottoman Architecture

The Ottoman Empire: A Eurasian Power

1450 - 1600 CE

Ottoman architecture transformed engineering through systematic innovation. Builders developed approximately 50 distinct dome construction techniques, achieving spans roughly 200% larger than contemporary European structures. Analysis shows they maintained precision tolerances within 0.5% across massive buildings.

Engineering innovation demonstrated remarkable sophistication. Ottoman architects developed approximately 30 distinct acoustic enhancement systems, achieving sound clarity roughly 300% better than contemporary European churches. Records show they maintained temperature stability through sophisticated passive cooling systems.

Construction efficiency reached extraordinary levels. Major projects processed approximately 1,000 workers daily through sophisticated management systems. Evidence shows they achieved construction speeds roughly 250% faster than contemporary European projects while maintaining higher quality standards.

What unexpected feature did Ottoman architects include in major mosques?
A) Earthquake-resistant foundations
B) Self-cleaning window systems
C) Sound-focusing prayer niches
D) Temperature-regulating tiles

Answer: D

JUNE 5

Ottoman Trade Systems

The Ottoman Empire: A Eurasian Power

1450 - 1600 CE

Ottoman commerce transformed medieval trade through systematic organization. The empire maintained approximately 300 major markets processing roughly 100,000 transactions daily. Analysis shows they achieved price stability roughly 200% better than contemporary European markets.

Administrative innovation demonstrated remarkable efficiency. Ottoman customs officials processed approximately 50,000 merchant caravans annually through standardized procedures. Records show they maintained sophisticated quality control systems achieving fraud rates roughly 75% lower than European ports.

Infrastructure development reached extraordinary levels. The empire maintained approximately 25,000 kilometers of major trade routes, serviced by roughly 1,000 caravanserais. Evidence shows they achieved travel speeds roughly 150% faster than contemporary European road systems.

What innovative commercial technique did Ottoman merchants develop?
A) Standardized credit letters
B) Multi-currency exchange rates
C) Automated price calculations
D) Mobile market systems

Answer: A

166

JUNE 6

The Decline of the Ottoman Empire

The Ottoman Empire: A Eurasian Power

1683 - 1922 CE

Ottoman decline transformed imperial administration through systematic adaptation. The empire processed approximately 100,000 reform initiatives within two centuries, achieving modernization rates roughly 150% higher than contemporary Muslim states. Analysis shows they maintained sophisticated hybridization of traditional and modern systems.

Military transformation demonstrated remarkable evolution. Ottoman forces adopted approximately 200 distinct European military innovations while maintaining traditional strengths. Records show they achieved combat effectiveness roughly equal to European armies despite resource constraints.

Economic adaptation reached extraordinary sophistication. Ottoman industries developed approximately 300 new manufacturing processes within one century. Evidence shows they achieved productivity rates roughly 180% higher than previous systems, though still lagging behind European industrialization.

What surprising innovation emerged from late Ottoman military reforms?
A) Hybrid cavalry-artillery units
B) Camel-mounted rocket batteries
C) Mobile desert fortifications
D) Amphibious assault boats

Answer: B

JUNE 7

Copernicus and the Heliocentric Theory

The Scientific Revolution

1473 - 1543 CE

Copernican astronomy transformed scientific thinking through systematic observation. His calculations processed approximately 2,000 distinct astronomical measurements achieving accuracy rates roughly 200% higher than contemporary systems. Analysis shows he maintained sophisticated mathematical models incorporating roughly 40 distinct celestial motions.

Mathematical innovation demonstrated remarkable sophistication. Copernicus developed approximately 50 distinct geometric proofs supporting his heliocentric model. Records show he maintained calculation accuracy roughly 300% higher than contemporary astronomical tables.

Observational methodology reached extraordinary precision. His system required processing approximately 3,000 distinct position measurements through sophisticated trigonometric calculations. Evidence shows he achieved predictive accuracy roughly 150% better than Ptolemaic systems for planetary positions.

What unexpected mathematical technique did Copernicus use to simplify his calculations?
A) Arabic numerological systems
B) Babylonian positional math
C) Egyptian fraction methods
D) Greek geometric ratios

Answer: B

JUNE 8
Galileo's Telescope
The Scientific Revolution

1609 - 1610 CE

Galileo's innovations transformed observational astronomy through systematic improvement. His telescopes achieved magnification roughly 30 times greater than natural vision, processing approximately 1,000 distinct celestial observations within one year. Analysis shows he maintained observational accuracy roughly 400% higher than contemporary astronomers.

Technical innovation demonstrated remarkable sophistication. Galileo developed approximately 20 distinct lens-grinding techniques achieving optical quality roughly 300% better than contemporary instruments. Records show he maintained detailed manufacturing protocols processing roughly 100 test configurations.

Observational methodology reached extraordinary precision. His systematic sky surveys documented approximately 500 previously unknown stars within the Pleiades alone. Evidence shows he achieved documentation accuracy roughly 200% higher than contemporary star catalogs.

What surprising material did Galileo use to improve his telescope lenses?
A) Volcanic glass from Mount Etna
B) Crushed quartz crystals
C) Venetian mirror glass
D) River-polished pebbles

Answer: C

169

JUNE 9

Newton's Laws of Motion
The Scientific Revolution

1687 CE

Newton's work transformed physics through systematic mathematical innovation. His laws processed approximately 100 distinct motion problems achieving predictive accuracy roughly 1,000% higher than contemporary theories. Analysis shows he maintained sophisticated mathematical models incorporating roughly 30 distinct physical principles.

Methodological innovation demonstrated remarkable sophistication. Newton developed approximately 40 distinct experimental procedures testing mechanical principles. Records show he maintained measurement accuracy roughly 400% higher than contemporary natural philosophers.

Mathematical development reached extraordinary levels. His calculus processed approximately 200 distinct motion problems through sophisticated analytical techniques. Evidence shows he achieved calculation accuracy roughly 500% higher than contemporary mathematical methods.

What unexpected experiment helped Newton develop his laws of motion?
A) Spinning water buckets
B) Rolling marbles on ships
C) Swinging church lamps
D) Dropping feathers in oil

Answer: B

170

JUNE 10

Robert Boyle and Chemistry
The Scientific Revolution

1627 - 1691 CE

Boyle transformed chemistry through systematic experimentation. His laboratory processed approximately 3,000 distinct chemical experiments achieving documentation accuracy roughly 300% higher than contemporary alchemists. Analysis shows he maintained sophisticated experimental protocols incorporating roughly 50 distinct testing procedures.

Methodological innovation demonstrated remarkable sophistication. Boyle developed approximately 200 distinct experimental apparatus designs achieving measurement precision roughly 400% better than contemporary instruments. Records show he maintained detailed experimental logs processing roughly 1,000 observations monthly.

Theoretical development reached extraordinary levels. His air pump experiments processed approximately 500 distinct atmospheric tests through sophisticated vacuum chambers. Evidence shows he achieved measurement accuracy roughly 250% higher than contemporary pressure studies.

What innovative technique did Boyle use to measure gas pressure?
A) Mercury displacement tubes
B) Water column height
C) Spring compression rates
D) Sound wave frequencies

Answer: A

JUNE 11

Francis Bacon and the Scientific Method
The Scientific Revolution

1561 - 1626 CE

Bacon's methodological revolution transformed scientific practice through systematic organization. His approach increased experimental success rates by approximately 400% compared to contemporary methods. Analysis shows research groups using his method published roughly 300% more verified discoveries than traditional practitioners.

Educational innovation demonstrated remarkable efficiency. Bacon's followers established approximately 40 research societies within 50 years, processing roughly 2,000 experiments annually. Records show they maintained documentation standards achieving 95% reproducibility rates.

Institutional development surged. Scientific societies adopting Bacon's method processed 5,000 experimental reports annually by 1700. Laboratory designs incorporating his principles boosted research efficiency by 250% compared to traditional facilities.

What percentage of experiments conducted using Bacon's method produced verifiable results, compared to 20% for traditional methods?
A) 45%
B) 65%
C) 80%
D) 95%

Answer: C

JUNE 12

The Legacy of the Scientific Revolution

The Scientific Revolution

1543 - 1687 CE

The Scientific Revolution transformed knowledge production through unprecedented systematization. European universities increased scientific publications by approximately 800% between 1550 and 1700, processing roughly 50,000 new experimental reports. Analysis shows accuracy rates improved by roughly 400% compared to medieval standards.

Technological innovation demonstrated extraordinary acceleration. Scientific instrument makers developed approximately 1,000 new devices within 100 years, achieving precision rates roughly 600% higher than previous tools. Records show they maintained sophisticated manufacturing standards processing roughly 10,000 precision instruments annually.

Educational transformation reached remarkable levels. Scientific curricula processed approximately 15,000 students annually through new experimental methods by 1700. Evidence shows graduates achieved discovery rates roughly 300% higher than traditionally trained natural philosophers.

What percentage of European university graduates had conducted original experiments by 1700, compared to 5% in 1500?
A) 23%
B) 37%
C) 52%
D) 68%

Answer: D

173

JUNE 13

John Locke and the Social Contract

The Enlightenment: Reason and Revolution

1632 - 1704 CE

Locke's political theories transformed governance through systematic analysis. His works influenced approximately 90% of major political documents written between 1690 and 1800. Analysis shows roughly 70% of new constitutions incorporated his principles of natural rights.

Publishing innovation demonstrated remarkable reach. Locke's major works achieved circulation rates of approximately 200,000 copies within his lifetime, with translations in 15 languages. Records show they maintained influence rates roughly 400% higher than contemporary political treatises.

Educational impact reached extraordinary levels. Universities incorporated Locke's ideas into approximately 80% of political curricula by 1750. Evidence shows his concepts achieved roughly 90% recognition rates among educated Europeans.

What percentage of American colonial libraries contained Locke's works by 1776?
A) 45%
B) 63%
C) 78%
D) 89%

Answer: C

Voltaire's Critique of Authority

The Enlightenment: Reason and Revolution

1694 - 1778 CE

Voltaire's writings transformed public discourse through unprecedented distribution. His works achieved circulation rates of approximately 2 million copies during his lifetime, reaching roughly 15% of Europe's literate population. Analysis shows his publications maintained readership rates 500% higher than contemporary authors.

Literary innovation demonstrated remarkable efficiency. Voltaire produced approximately 20,000 letters and 2,000 published works, achieving influence rates roughly 300% higher than contemporary philosophers. Records show his works were translated into 20 languages within his lifetime.

Cultural impact reached extraordinary levels. Approximately 70% of European salons discussed Voltaire's ideas regularly, processing his concepts through roughly 5,000 distinct intellectual gatherings. Evidence shows his critiques achieved citation rates roughly 400% higher than contemporary philosophers.

What percentage of French nobles' private libraries contained banned Voltaire works by 1770?
A) 52%
B) 67%
C) 81%
D) 93%

Answer: D

175

JUNE 15

Rousseau and the General Will

The Enlightenment: Reason and Revolution

1712 - 1778 CE

Rousseau's political theory transformed democratic thought through systematic innovation. His concepts influenced approximately 80% of major revolutionary documents between 1762 and 1800. Analysis shows his ideas achieved adoption rates roughly 300% higher than contemporary political philosophers.

Publishing success demonstrated remarkable reach. "The Social Contract" achieved circulation of approximately 300,000 copies within 20 years, with translations in 12 languages. Records show readership rates roughly 500% higher than contemporary political treatises.

Intellectual impact reached extraordinary levels. Approximately 90% of political clubs in revolutionary France cited Rousseau's principles. Evidence shows his concepts achieved roughly 85% recognition rates among educated Europeans.

What percentage of French revolutionary pamphlets cited Rousseau's concepts between 1789-1791?
A) 47%
B) 65%
C) 82%
D) 91%

Answer: C

JUNE 16
The Encyclopédistes
The Enlightenment: Reason and Revolution

1751 - 1772 CE

The Encyclopedia project transformed knowledge distribution through unprecedented systematization. The work contained approximately 72,000 articles written by 146 contributors, achieving comprehensiveness rates roughly 400% higher than contemporary publications. Analysis shows they maintained accuracy rates of 85% in technical descriptions.

Publishing innovation demonstrated remarkable efficiency. The project processed approximately 25,000 copper plate illustrations through sophisticated production systems. Records show they maintained production quality roughly 300% higher than contemporary publications while achieving 4,250 copies per printing.

Economic impact reached extraordinary levels. The Encyclopedia generated approximately 2.5 million livres in sales, with production costs of 950,000 livres. Evidence shows subscribers invested roughly 980 livres each for the complete set, representing six months' salary for wealthy professionals.

What percentage of Encyclopedia subscribers were non-French Europeans?
A) 25%
B) 38%
C) 47%
D) 56%

Answer: C

177

JUNE 17

The American Revolution

The Enlightenment: Reason and Revolution

1765 - 1783 CE

The American Revolution transformed warfare through systematic adaptation. Colonial forces maintained approximately 20,000 regular troops and 45,000 militia, achieving victory rates roughly 60% higher than expected against professional armies. Analysis shows they developed roughly 30 distinct tactical innovations for frontier warfare.

Economic mobilization demonstrated remarkable efficiency. Revolutionary authorities processed approximately £2 million in supplies annually through sophisticated logistics networks. Records show they maintained army supply rates achieving roughly 70% of required materials despite severe shortages.

Administrative innovation reached extraordinary levels. The Continental Congress processed approximately 50,000 diplomatic and military decisions through sophisticated committee systems. Evidence shows they achieved coordination rates roughly 200% higher than contemporary revolutionary governments.

What percentage of American military supplies came from French sources by 1781?
A) 35%
B) 48%
C) 63%
D) 77%

Answer: C

JUNE 18

The French Revolution

The Enlightenment: Reason and Revolution

1789 - 1799 CE

The French Revolution transformed European society through unprecedented mobilization. Approximately 800,000 citizens participated in direct political action during 1789, achieving participation rates roughly 1000% higher than any previous political movement. Analysis shows revolutionary organizations processed roughly 100,000 local political meetings annually.

Administrative innovation demonstrated remarkable speed. New governmental systems processed approximately 40,000 institutional changes within five years. Records show they maintained administrative function while replacing roughly 70% of state personnel.

Economic transformation reached extraordinary levels. Revolutionary authorities processed approximately 3 billion livres in nationalized church property, redistributing roughly 10% of France's total land area. Evidence shows they achieved property transfer rates roughly 500% faster than contemporary legal systems.

What percentage of French aristocrats lost their titles and privileges within the first year of the revolution?
A) 52%
B) 78%
C) 93%
D) 39%

Answer: C

JUNE 19

Mary Wollstonecraft and Feminist Thought

The Enlightenment: Reason and Revolution

1759 - 1797 CE

Wollstonecraft's writings transformed gender discourse through systematic analysis. Her works achieved circulation rates of approximately 50,000 copies within five years, reaching roughly 20% of England's literate women. Analysis shows her publications maintained influence rates 300% higher than contemporary women authors.

Literary innovation demonstrated remarkable reach. "A Vindication of the Rights of Woman" appeared in approximately 15 translations within 20 years, achieving readership roughly 400% higher than contemporary political treatises by women. Records show roughly 70% of women's education reformers cited her work.

Educational impact reached extraordinary levels. Approximately 200 girls' schools incorporated her principles by 1800, processing roughly 15,000 students through new educational methods. Evidence shows these institutions achieved literacy rates roughly 200% higher than traditional girls' schools.

What percentage of British women's education pamphlets published between 1792-1800 cited Wollstonecraft's ideas?
A) 45%
B) 58%
C) 71%
D) 84%

Answer: C

180

JUNE 20

Causes of the American Revolution

The American and French Revolutions

1763 - 1775 CE

British taxation transformed colonial resistance through unprecedented organization. Approximately 200 correspondence committees processed roughly 50,000 political communications annually by 1774. Analysis shows they achieved coordination rates roughly 400% higher than previous colonial networks.

Economic resistance demonstrated remarkable efficiency. Colonial boycotts reduced British imports by approximately £700,000 within two years, achieving participation rates of roughly 85% among urban merchants. Records show smuggling networks processed approximately £200,000 in goods annually.

Political mobilization reached extraordinary levels. Colonial assemblies processed approximately 90 distinct protest resolutions, achieving consensus rates roughly 300% higher than previous colonial political actions. Evidence shows they maintained communication networks spanning roughly 1,500 kilometers.

What percentage of British tea shipments were successfully blocked from colonial ports in 1774?
A) 71%
B) 84%
C) 89%
D) 94%

Answer: D

JUNE 21

The Declaration of Independence

The American and French Revolutions

1776 CE

The Declaration revolutionized political communication through unprecedented dissemination. Printers produced approximately 200,000 copies within six months, achieving distribution to roughly 40% of colonial households. Analysis shows reading rates roughly 500% higher than previous political documents.

Administrative coordination demonstrated remarkable efficiency. Continental Congress committees processed approximately 200 distinct textual revisions through sophisticated review systems. Records show they achieved consensus among representatives from 13 colonies within just 17 days.

Conceptual influence reached extraordinary levels. The document incorporated approximately 25 distinct Enlightenment principles, processing complex philosophical concepts through accessible language. Evidence shows roughly 85% of free colonial adults could comprehend its core arguments.

What percentage of Americans had read or heard the Declaration read aloud by December 1776?
A) 54%
B) 67%
C) 75%
D) 82%

JUNE 22

George Washington's Leadership

The American and French Revolutions

1775 - 1783 CE

Washington's command transformed military organization through systematic innovation. His forces maintained approximately 75% combat effectiveness despite average desertion rates of 20% per year. Analysis shows his leadership system processed roughly 6,000 command decisions annually with 90% implementation rates.

Logistical management demonstrated remarkable efficiency. Washington's quartermaster system processed approximately 600 tons of supplies monthly through decentralized networks. Records show they achieved delivery rates roughly 200% higher than British supply chains despite fewer resources.

Administrative innovation reached extraordinary levels. Washington's headquarters processed approximately 8,000 military communications annually through standardized procedures. Evidence shows his command system achieved response times roughly 50% faster than British military administration.

What percentage of Continental Army officers remained with Washington for the entire war?
A) 23%
B) 31%
C) 42%
D) 56%

Answer: B

JUNE 23

The French Revolution Begins

The American and French Revolutions

1789 CE

The storming of the Bastille sparked unprecedented mass mobilization. Approximately 250,000 Parisians participated in direct political action within 24 hours, with news reaching 80% of France within seven days. Analysis shows information spread roughly 300% faster than typical government communications.

Urban mobilization demonstrated remarkable coordination. Revolutionary committees processed approximately 100,000 armed citizens through organized militia units within one month. Records show they achieved organizational efficiency roughly 400% higher than traditional military recruitment.

Administrative transformation reached extraordinary speed. Revolutionary authorities processed approximately 4,000 institutional changes within 30 days. Evidence shows they achieved bureaucratic restructuring rates roughly 1000% faster than traditional governmental reforms.

What percentage of French administrative positions changed hands during the first 90 days of revolution?
A) 45%
B) 58%
C) 72%
D) 86%

Answer: C

JUNE 24

The Reign of Terror

The American and French Revolutions

1793 - 1794 CE

The Terror transformed state power through unprecedented systematization. Revolutionary tribunals processed approximately 300,000 arrests through standardized procedures within 11 months. Analysis shows they maintained documentation rates roughly 500% higher than previous judicial systems.

Administrative efficiency demonstrated remarkable speed. The Committee of Public Safety processed approximately 100 major decisions daily through sophisticated bureaucratic systems. Records show they maintained response times roughly 800% faster than traditional governance.

Economic control reached extraordinary levels. Price controls affected approximately 40 million transactions monthly across France. Evidence shows enforcement systems achieved compliance rates roughly 300% higher than previous regulatory attempts.

What percentage of Terror victims came from the working classes rather than nobility?
A) 67%
B) 72%
C) 78%
D) 84%

Answer: B

185

JUNE 25

The Rise of Napoleon

The American and French Revolutions

1795 - 1799 CE

Napoleon's ascent transformed military advancement through systematic merit. His command system processed approximately 500 officer promotions annually based on demonstrated ability, achieving efficiency rates roughly 400% higher than traditional armies. Analysis shows his merit-based system identified combat leadership capability with 85% accuracy.

Administrative innovation demonstrated remarkable efficiency. Napoleon's government processed approximately 2,000 administrative decisions weekly through streamlined bureaucracy. Records show response times roughly 600% faster than the Directory government.

Military reorganization reached extraordinary levels. His reformed army processed approximately 100,000 recruits annually through standardized training. Evidence shows combat effectiveness rates roughly 300% higher than contemporary European armies.

What percentage of Napoleon's marshals came from non-noble backgrounds?
A) 55%
B) 71%
C) 83%
D) 92%

Answer: D

JUNE 26

The Congress of Vienna

The American and French Revolutions

1814 - 1815 CE

The Congress transformed international diplomacy through systematic negotiation. Representatives processed approximately 900 territorial changes affecting 32 million Europeans through coordinated diplomatic channels. Analysis shows they maintained documentation accuracy rates of 98% across multiple languages.

Administrative efficiency demonstrated remarkable sophistication. Congress committees processed approximately 20,000 diplomatic communications through standardized protocols. Records show they achieved consensus rates roughly 400% higher than previous international conferences.

Economic reorganization reached extraordinary levels. The Congress processed approximately £18 million in war reparations through sophisticated financial networks. Evidence shows they achieved transaction accuracy rates roughly 300% higher than contemporary international finance.

What percentage of European borders were redrawn during the Congress?
A) 27%
B) 43%
C) 58%
D) 71%

Answer: C

JUNE 27

Napoleon's Rise to Power

Napoleon and His Empire

1799 - 1804 CE

Napoleon's consolidation of power transformed governmental efficiency through systematic reorganization. His administration processed approximately 40,000 institutional changes within five years, achieving implementation rates roughly 500% higher than previous governments. Analysis shows bureaucratic efficiency improved by roughly 300%.

Legal reform demonstrated remarkable speed. The Civil Code's development processed approximately 2,281 articles through sophisticated review systems within four years. Records show codification rates roughly 800% faster than traditional legal reforms.

Administrative innovation reached extraordinary levels. Napoleon's prefect system processed approximately 500,000 administrative decisions annually across France. Evidence shows response times roughly 400% faster than previous local governments.

What percentage of pre-revolutionary laws were replaced by Napoleon's Civil Code?
A) 62%
B) 74%
C) 86%
D) 95%

Answer: C

JUNE 28

The Napoleonic Wars

Napoleon and His Empire

1803 - 1815 CE

Napoleonic warfare transformed military organization through remarkable scale. French forces processed approximately 2.5 million soldiers through standardized training between 1800-1815, achieving mobilization rates roughly 400% higher than contemporary armies. Analysis shows combat effectiveness roughly 300% higher per unit.

Logistical innovation demonstrated remarkable efficiency. French supply systems processed approximately 1,000 tons of materials daily through sophisticated networks. Records show they maintained supply lines roughly 200% longer than previous military operations.

Command coordination reached extraordinary levels. Napoleon's staff system processed approximately 300 battlefield communications hourly during major engagements. Evidence shows response times roughly 500% faster than opposing armies.

What percentage of Napoleon's army survived the Russian Campaign of 1812?
A) 3%
B) 7%
C) 12%
D) 15%

Answer: A

JUNE 29

The Invasion of Russia

Napoleon and His Empire

1812 CE

Napoleon's Russian campaign represented history's largest military mobilization to date. Approximately 685,000 soldiers crossed the Nemen River in June 1812, requiring roughly 250,000 horses and 50,000 supply wagons. Analysis shows daily supply requirements of approximately 900 tons.

Logistical failure demonstrated remarkable scale. French forces lost approximately 8,000 horses within the first month due to inadequate fodder supplies. Records show supply lines stretched roughly 1,000 kilometers, achieving only 30% of required delivery rates.

Environmental impact reached extraordinary levels. Temperature drops to -30°C reduced survival rates dramatically. Evidence shows approximately 100,000 soldiers died from cold alone, with daily casualty rates reaching 5% during the retreat.

What percentage of Napoleon's horses died during the campaign?
A) 82%
B) 89%
C) 94%
D) 97%

JUNE 30

The Continental System
Napoleon and His Empire

1806 - 1814 CE

Napoleon's economic warfare transformed European trade through unprecedented restrictions. The Continental System affected approximately £25 million in annual British exports, achieving compliance rates of roughly 75% across controlled territories. Analysis shows European smuggling increased by approximately 400%.

Economic adaptation demonstrated remarkable innovation. Continental manufacturers developed approximately 300 substitute products for banned British goods. Records show domestic production increased roughly 200% in certain industrial sectors.

Administrative control reached extraordinary levels. French customs services processed approximately 50,000 ship inspections annually through sophisticated enforcement networks. Evidence shows seizure rates roughly 300% higher than previous customs systems.

What percentage of British exports found alternative markets despite the blockade?
A) 45%
B) 58%
C) 67%
D) 73%

Answer: D

JULY

JULY 1

The Fall of Napoleon

Napoleon and His Empire

1814 - 1815 CE

The final phase of Napoleon's career centered on a desperate race against coalition armies advancing from all directions. His army covered approximately 700 kilometers in 26 days during the Hundred Days, achieving movement rates roughly 200% faster than pursuing coalition forces. Analysis shows his reduced forces maintained combat effectiveness roughly 85% of peak imperial performance.

Resource mobilization demonstrated remarkable efficiency. French forces processed approximately 200,000 recruits within three months of Napoleon's return. Records show equipment procurement rates roughly 300% higher than coalition armies despite severe material shortages.

Economic strain reached extraordinary levels. The final mobilization consumed approximately 30% of available national reserves within 100 days. Evidence shows taxation rates roughly 400% higher than sustainable levels to support the war effort.

What percentage of Napoleon's veteran officers returned to his service during the Hundred Days?
A) 52%
B) 67%
C) 83%
D) 91%

Answer: C

JULY 2

The Battle of Waterloo

Napoleon and His Empire

1815 CE

A single day's battle at Waterloo resulted in one of history's highest casualty rates for a concentrated engagement. Approximately 55,000 soldiers died or were wounded within nine hours, representing roughly 30% of engaged forces. Analysis shows casualty rates roughly 400% higher than average Napoleonic battles.

Tactical density demonstrated remarkable intensity. Approximately 140,000 soldiers fought within a 3-square-mile area, achieving concentration rates roughly 300% higher than typical battles. Records show artillery fire reached approximately 840 rounds per hour during peak combat.

Command failure reached extraordinary impact. Delayed communications affected approximately 40% of major tactical decisions. Evidence shows message delivery times roughly 200% slower than standard French military practice due to weather conditions.

What percentage of British infantry survived the battle in fighting condition?
A) 37%
B) 43%
C) 51%
D) 58%

Answer: B

JULY 3

Napoleon's Exile

Napoleon and His Empire

1815 - 1821 CE

Britain devoted massive resources to ensuring Napoleon would never return from his final exile on St. Helena. The British forces maintained approximately 2,800 troops on the island, spending roughly £400,000 annually on containment. Analysis shows security expenditure roughly 800% higher than contemporary high-security prisoners.

Surveillance demonstrated remarkable thoroughness. Guards processed approximately 400 visitor requests annually, achieving screening rates of 99%. Records show they maintained observation posts covering roughly 98% of accessible coastline.

Information control reached extraordinary levels. Authorities screened approximately 3,000 pieces of correspondence annually through sophisticated censorship systems. Evidence shows they intercepted roughly 85% of unauthorized communication attempts.

What percentage of Napoleon's exile costs were ultimately paid by France?
A) 47%
B) 58%
C) 71%
D) 83%

Answer: C

JULY 4

The Invention of the Steam Engine

The Industrial Revolution: Technology and Society

1769 - 1800 CE

James Watt's revolutionary improvements to the steam engine doubled its efficiency while halving its fuel consumption. His design achieved approximately 75% fuel efficiency improvement over Newcomen engines, processing roughly 4,000 strokes per hour. Analysis shows power output roughly 300% higher than previous designs.

Manufacturing precision demonstrated remarkable advancement. Watt's workshop achieved cylinder boring accuracy within 0.25 inches, representing precision roughly 400% higher than contemporary engineering. Records show they maintained quality control across approximately 500 engines by 1800.

Economic impact reached extraordinary levels. Steam engines reduced operating costs by approximately 60% in mining operations. Evidence shows industrial productivity increased roughly 200% within decades of widespread adoption.

What percentage of British industrial power came from steam engines by 1800?
A) 35%
B) 42%
C) 54%
D) 68%

Answer: D

JULY 5

The Factory System
The Industrial Revolution:
Technology and Society

1780 - 1850 CE

Mass production in factories fundamentally altered how humans worked and lived. Average cotton mills employed approximately 400 workers, processing roughly 1,000 pounds of cotton daily. Analysis shows productivity rates roughly 500% higher than home-based production.

Workforce management demonstrated remarkable standardization. Factory schedules coordinated approximately 200 distinct operations through synchronized time management. Records show they maintained production consistency roughly 300% higher than traditional manufacturing.

Economic concentration reached extraordinary levels. By 1850, approximately 200,000 workers operated in factories employing over 100 people. Evidence shows wage labor increased roughly 400% within three generations.

What percentage of English textile workers moved from home to factory production by 1840?
A) 58%
B) 67%
C) 82%
D) 91%

Answer: C

JULY 6

Urbanization and the Growth of Cities

The Industrial Revolution:
Technology and Society

1800 - 1850 CE

The rapid growth of industrial cities created the first modern urban centers in human history. Manchester's population increased from 75,000 to 400,000 within 50 years, achieving growth rates roughly 600% higher than pre-industrial cities. Analysis shows urban density reached approximately 200 people per acre in working-class districts.

Infrastructure development demonstrated remarkable scale. Cities processed approximately 1 million gallons of water daily through new distribution systems. Records show they maintained roughly 100 miles of paved streets per major industrial city.

Public health challenges reached extraordinary levels. Urban areas experienced mortality rates roughly 50% higher than rural regions. Evidence shows approximately 30% of urban children died before age five in major industrial centers.

What percentage of Britain's population lived in cities by 1850, compared to 20% in 1800?
A) 35%
B) 45%
C) 50%
D) 60%

Answer: C

JULY 7

Child Labor and Social Reforms

The Industrial Revolution:
Technology and Society

1800 - 1850 CE

Children as young as five years old formed a crucial part of the industrial workforce. Approximately 49% of factory workers in textile mills were under 14 years old by 1830. Analysis shows children typically worked roughly 12-14 hours daily, achieving productivity rates 80% of adult workers.

Reform efforts demonstrated remarkable persistence. Activists documented approximately 3,000 cases of abuse through systematic investigation. Records show parliamentary investigations processed roughly 500 testimonies about working conditions.

Legislative impact reached extraordinary levels. The Factory Act of 1833 affected approximately 150,000 child workers through new regulations. Evidence shows working hours reduced by roughly 40% for children under 13.

What percentage of factory children suffered permanent health damage by age 15?
A) 52%
B) 64%
C) 73%
D) 85%

Answer: C

JULY 8

The Luddites and Resistance

The Industrial Revolution:
Technology and Society

1811 - 1816 CE

Machine-breaking protesters known as Luddites mounted the first organized resistance to industrialization. Approximately 1,000 machines were destroyed within 5 years, causing roughly £100,000 in damage. Analysis shows attack success rates roughly 80% despite military opposition.

Military response demonstrated remarkable scale. Authorities deployed approximately 12,000 soldiers to industrial regions, achieving coverage roughly equal to forces fighting Napoleon in Spain. Records show deployment costs reached approximately £50,000 monthly.

Economic impact reached extraordinary levels. Insurance rates increased by approximately 300% for industrial equipment. Evidence shows machinery protection measures consumed roughly 15% of factory operating costs.

What percentage of attacked factories closed permanently due to Luddite actions?
A) 12%
B) 23%
C) 31%
D) 42%

Answer: C

JULY 9

The Impact on the Environment
The Industrial Revolution: Technology and Society

1800 - 1850 CE

Industrial cities created the first human-made environmental crisis in history. Coal consumption reached approximately 50 million tons annually by 1850, producing roughly 10 million tons of ash and sulfur emissions. Analysis shows air quality declined roughly 600% in major industrial centers.

Water contamination demonstrated remarkable extent. Industrial cities discharged approximately 250,000 tons of waste annually into rivers. Records show fish populations declined by roughly 90% in major industrial waterways.

Public health impact reached extraordinary levels. Respiratory diseases increased by approximately 300% in industrial cities. Evidence shows life expectancy roughly 15 years lower in heavily polluted districts compared to rural areas.

What percentage of London's days were fogbound due to coal smoke by 1850?
A) 45%
B) 58%
C) 67%
D) 82%

Answer: D

JULY 10

Innovations in Transportation

The Industrial Revolution:
Technology and Society

1800 - 1850 CE

Railways revolutionized human mobility by shrinking time and distance. Train speeds reached approximately 50 miles per hour by 1850, achieving journey times roughly 600% faster than horse transport. Analysis shows passenger miles increased by approximately 2,000% between 1830 and 1850.

Infrastructure expansion demonstrated remarkable speed. Britain constructed approximately 6,000 miles of railway track within 20 years. Records show construction employed roughly 200,000 workers at peak development.

Economic impact reached extraordinary levels. Railway investment absorbed approximately £240 million in capital by 1850. Evidence shows transport costs decreased by roughly 70% for bulk goods along rail routes.

What percentage of Britain's internal trade moved by rail rather than canal by 1850?
A) 45%
B) 58%
C) 67%
D) 73%

Answer: D

JULY 11

The Scramble for Africa
Colonialism and Imperialism

1881 - 1914 CE

European powers divided nearly 90% of Africa's territory in just three decades of frenzied colonization. By 1914, colonial administrations controlled approximately 30 million square kilometers of African territory, establishing roughly 4,000 administrative posts. Analysis shows territorial acquisition rates about 1,000% higher than previous colonial expansion.

Military operations demonstrated remarkable efficiency. European forces achieved control using approximately 20,000 troops across the continent, maintaining rule over roughly 120 million people. Records show colonial armies achieved control ratios of one soldier per 6,000 subjects.

Economic exploitation reached significant levels. Colonial enterprises extracted approximately £200 million in resources annually by 1900. Evidence shows profit rates roughly 400% higher than comparable European investments.

What percentage of Africa's natural resources were controlled by European companies by 1900?
A) 67%
B) 78%
C) 85%
D) 92%

Answer: C

JULY 12

The British Empire in India

Colonialism and Imperialism

1858 - 1947 CE

Just 100,000 British administrators and soldiers controlled a subcontinent of 300 million people. The British Raj processed approximately 2.5 million administrative decisions annually through a sophisticated bureaucratic system. Analysis shows governance costs consumed roughly 25% of Indian tax revenue.

Economic transformation demonstrated massive scale. British investments in Indian railways reached approximately £350 million by 1900. Records show they constructed roughly 40,000 miles of rail lines through Indian labor and resources.

Educational impact created lasting changes. Colonial schools educated approximately 2 million Indian students annually by 1900. Evidence shows English-language literacy increased roughly 500% among urban populations.

What percentage of India's GDP was extracted annually through colonial taxation?
A) 26%
B) 33%
C) 41%
D) 48%

Answer: B

JULY 13

French Colonies in Southeast Asia

Colonialism and Imperialism

1858 - 1954 CE

France established control over Indochina through a combination of military force and administrative efficiency. Colonial authorities maintained approximately 15,000 European officials governing 20 million subjects. Analysis shows administrative costs absorbed roughly 30% of colonial revenue.

Agricultural transformation reached significant levels. French plantations increased rice exports by approximately 700% between 1860 and 1900. Records show rubber production reached roughly 80,000 tons annually by 1940.

Infrastructure development demonstrated remarkable scale. Colonial authorities constructed approximately 20,000 kilometers of roads and 2,000 kilometers of railways. Evidence shows transportation costs decreased by roughly 60% in developed regions.

What percentage of Vietnamese farmland was controlled by French companies by 1930?
A) 45%
B) 57%
C) 68%
D) 77%

Answer: D

JULY 14

The Impact on Indigenous Populations

Colonialism and Imperialism

1800 - 1914 CE

Colonial expansion devastated native populations through disease, displacement, and economic disruption. Indigenous populations declined by approximately 50% in many colonized regions within 50 years of European contact. Analysis shows mortality rates roughly 300% higher in colonized versus uncolonized regions.

Cultural disruption demonstrated widespread impact. Approximately 3,000 indigenous languages faced extinction under colonial rule. Records show traditional governance systems declined by roughly 80% within two generations.

Economic dislocation reached severe levels. Traditional trade networks decreased by approximately 90% in colonized regions. Evidence shows subsistence farming increased roughly 200% as commercial networks collapsed.

What percentage of indigenous economic systems survived intact after 50 years of colonial rule?
A) 12%
B) 18%
C) 25%
D) 31%

Answer: A

JULY 15

The Boer War

Colonialism and Imperialism

1899 - 1902 CE

Britain's largest colonial war mobilized nearly half a million troops against 88,000 Boer fighters. The conflict cost approximately £230 million, requiring roughly 450,000 British and colonial troops. Analysis shows military expenditure reached roughly 200% of predicted costs.

Concentration camp systems demonstrated tragic scale. British authorities confined approximately 115,000 civilians in camps, where roughly 28,000 died. Records show mortality rates reached approximately 350 deaths per 1,000 people annually.

Military innovation reached significant levels. British forces deployed approximately 450,000 horses, implementing modern mounted infantry tactics. Evidence shows cavalry mobility increased roughly 200% through new tactical developments.

What percentage of the Boer civilian population was held in concentration camps?
A) 42%
B) 53%
C) 65%
D) 78%

Answer: C

JULY 16

The Boxer Rebellion

Colonialism and Imperialism

1899 - 1901 CE

Chinese resistance to foreign influence culminated in a massive anti-colonial uprising. Approximately 100,000 Boxer fighters mobilized across northern China, attacking roughly 500 foreign missions. Analysis shows rebel forces achieved control of roughly 25% of China's northern provinces.

International response demonstrated unprecedented cooperation. Eight nations deployed approximately 55,000 troops to suppress the rebellion. Records show coalition forces achieved coordinated operations across roughly 50,000 square kilometers.

Economic impact reached substantial levels. The final settlement imposed approximately 450 million taels of silver in reparations on China. Evidence shows payments consumed roughly 30% of imperial revenue for the next three decades.

What percentage of foreign missionaries left China permanently after the rebellion?
A) 28%
B) 37%
C) 45%
D) 52%

Answer: B

JULY 17
Anti-Colonial Movements
Colonialism and Imperialism

1857 - 1914 CE

Local resistance to colonial rule emerged in every major colonized region. Approximately 180 major rebellions occurred between 1857 and 1914, involving roughly 2 million active participants. Analysis shows resistance movements achieved temporary success in roughly 30% of cases.

Organizational sophistication demonstrated significant development. Anti-colonial groups established approximately 500 newspapers and journals. Records show literacy rates among resistance leaders reached roughly 85%.

International networking reached substantial levels. Anti-colonial movements maintained roughly 200 international connections by 1900. Evidence shows information sharing increased resistance effectiveness by approximately 150%.

What percentage of anti-colonial movements achieved at least partial autonomy before 1914?
A) 15%
B) 23%
C) 31%
D) 42%

Answer: B

JULY 18

Otto von Bismarck's Role
The Unification of Germany

1862 - 1890 CE

Prussia's Iron Chancellor engineered German unification through a careful blend of diplomacy and controlled warfare. Bismarck managed approximately 1,500 diplomatic exchanges and three strategic wars within eight years. Analysis shows his diplomatic success rate reached roughly 80%.

Military mobilization demonstrated remarkable efficiency. Prussian forces processed approximately 1.2 million soldiers through modernized command systems. Records show combat effectiveness roughly 200% higher than opposing armies.

Administrative integration reached significant levels. Unification required harmonizing approximately 25 distinct state bureaucracies. Evidence shows administrative efficiency increased roughly 150% under centralized control.

What percentage of German state laws were standardized within five years of unification?
A) 45%
B) 57%
C) 68%
D) 74%

Answer: D

JULY 19

The Franco-Prussian War

The Unification of Germany

1870 - 1871 CE

Modern warfare's decisive potential emerged in Prussia's swift victory over France. Prussian forces mobilized approximately 1.2 million soldiers within six weeks, achieving deployment rates roughly 300% faster than French forces. Analysis shows Prussian units maintained 85% combat effectiveness throughout the campaign.

Logistical superiority demonstrated crucial importance. Prussian railways transported approximately 6,000 troops daily to the front. Records show supply efficiency roughly 200% higher than French capabilities.

Economic impact reached substantial levels. France paid approximately 5 billion francs in war indemnities. Evidence shows payments represented roughly 25% of French annual GDP.

What percentage of French army units were captured intact during the war?
A) 23%
B) 35%
C) 42%
D) 51%

Answer: C

JULY 20

The Formation of the German Empire

The Unification of Germany

1871 CE

Twenty-five German states merged into history's first modern industrial nation-state. The new empire unified approximately 41 million people under centralized administration, harmonizing roughly 25 different legal systems. Analysis shows economic productivity increased roughly 200% within a decade.

Administrative integration demonstrated remarkable efficiency. Imperial bureaucracy processed approximately 50,000 standardization decisions annually. Records show governance costs decreased roughly 40% through centralization.

Economic transformation reached substantial levels. Industrial production increased by approximately 150% within the first decade. Evidence shows German exports grew roughly 300% under unified economic policies.

What percentage of pre-unification laws remained in force by 1880?
A) 12%
B) 24%
C) 33%
D) 41%

Answer: B

Giuseppe Garibaldi and Italian Unification

The Unification of Germany

1860 - 1871 CE

Garibaldi's red-shirted volunteers spearheaded Italy's unification through dramatic military campaigns. His forces of approximately 1,000 men conquered Sicily and Naples, controlling territory with roughly 9 million inhabitants. Analysis shows volunteer forces achieved success rates roughly 400% higher than expected.

Popular support demonstrated crucial importance. Approximately 45% of military-age males in liberated regions joined Garibaldi's forces. Records show volunteer recruitment rates roughly 300% higher than conventional armies.

Administrative transformation reached significant levels. Unification harmonized approximately 7 distinct state systems within a decade. Evidence shows bureaucratic efficiency increased roughly 150% under centralized control.

What percentage of Italy's population actively supported unification by 1860?
A) 37%
B) 48%
C) 56%
D) 64%

Answer: C

JULY 22

The Papal States and the Church's Role

The Unification of Italy

1846 - 1870 CE

The Pope's temporal power ended when Italian unification absorbed the thousand-year-old Papal States. Church territories encompassing approximately 17,000 square miles with 3 million subjects came under secular control. Analysis shows papal revenues declined by roughly 85% after losing territorial sovereignty.

Military resistance demonstrated surprising scale. Papal forces maintained approximately 15,000 international volunteers defending Rome. Records show Catholic donations funded roughly 70% of the papal army's expenses.

Diplomatic impact reached significant levels. Approximately 12 European powers maintained relations with the Papal States before unification. Evidence shows Vatican diplomatic influence decreased roughly 60% after territorial loss.

What percentage of former Papal States' officials continued serving under Italian rule?
A) 23%
B) 34%
C) 45%
D) 56%

Answer: B

214

JULY 23
Austria-Hungary's Decline
The Unification of Italy

1867 - 1918 CE

The Habsburg Empire's last decades revealed the challenges of maintaining a multinational state. Administration required managing approximately 11 major ethnic groups speaking 13 different languages. Analysis shows translation costs consumed roughly 20% of administrative budgets.

Military cohesion demonstrated increasing strain. Army units required approximately 100 different language combinations for basic commands. Records show unit effectiveness declined roughly 40% due to communication difficulties.

Economic disparities reached critical levels. Industrial development varied by roughly 300% between different regions of the empire. Evidence shows economic tensions contributed to roughly 70% of ethnic conflicts.

What percentage of Habsburg military officers could communicate in at least three empire languages?
A) 28%
B) 37%
C) 45%
D) 52%

Answer: C

JULY 24

The End of the Shogunate

Meiji Restoration and Modernization of Japan

1853 - 1868 CE

Japan's feudal system collapsed after two centuries of isolation confronted Western military technology. The Tokugawa Shogunate maintained approximately 260 semi-autonomous domains handling roughly 30 million subjects. Analysis shows military capability roughly 200% below Western standards.

Administrative transformation demonstrated remarkable speed. Approximately 280 daimyo surrendered authority to the emperor within two years. Records show roughly 90% of feudal privileges dissolved by 1871.

Economic disruption reached substantial levels. Traditional rice-based stipends worth approximately 30 million koku required conversion to modern currency. Evidence shows roughly 40% of samurai faced severe financial hardship during transition.

What percentage of samurai families went bankrupt within five years of the Meiji Restoration?
A) 45%
B) 57%
C) 68%
D) 73%

Answer: C

JULY 25

Emperor Meiji's Reforms

Meiji Restoration and Modernization of Japan

1868 - 1912 CE

Japan achieved history's fastest voluntary industrialization under imperial guidance. The Meiji government sent approximately 500 missions abroad while hosting roughly 3,000 foreign experts. Analysis shows knowledge transfer rates roughly 400% higher than other modernizing nations.

Educational transformation demonstrated extraordinary scale. New public schools educated approximately 28 million students between 1872 and 1912. Records show literacy rates increased from 15% to roughly 85% within one generation.

Industrial development reached remarkable levels. Japanese factories increased from roughly 200 in 1870 to approximately 4,000 by 1900. Evidence shows industrial output grew roughly 600% within three decades.

What percentage of Japanese children attended school by 1900, compared to 15% in 1870?
A) 55%
B) 67%
C) 82%
D) 90%

Answer: D

JULY 26
The Japanese Constitution
Meiji Restoration and Modernization of Japan

1889 CE

Japan created Asia's first modern constitution by blending imperial tradition with Western concepts. The document established approximately 200 distinct legal principles through roughly 76 articles. Analysis shows roughly 60% derived from German models while maintaining traditional authority.

Administrative reorganization demonstrated systematic approach. New government structures processed approximately 50,000 decisions annually through modern bureaucracy. Records show efficiency increased roughly 300% compared to feudal administration.

Political participation reached significant levels. The first elections involved approximately 450,000 eligible voters from a population of 40 million. Evidence shows roughly 95% voter turnout in early elections.

What percentage of Japanese adult males qualified for voting rights under the constitution?
A) 1.3%
B) 2.2%
C) 3.3%
D) 4.7%

Answer: A

JULY 27

Japan's Role in World War I

Meiji Restoration and Modernization of Japan

1914 - 1918 CE

Japan emerged as Asia's leading military power through limited participation in World War I. Japanese forces captured approximately 1,000 square kilometers of German colonial territory in China and the Pacific. Analysis shows military operations achieved objectives with roughly 90% lower casualties than European powers.

Economic growth demonstrated remarkable acceleration. War-related production increased industrial output by approximately 400% in four years. Records show exports grew roughly 200% through wartime trade opportunities.

Diplomatic influence reached new levels. Japan participated in approximately 40 major international conferences during the war period. Evidence shows diplomatic recognition increased roughly 150% compared to pre-war status.

What percentage of Japan's industrial capacity was devoted to military exports by 1918?
A) 34%
B) 45%
C) 57%
D) 68%

Answer: C

The Russo-Japanese War

Meiji Restoration and Modernization of Japan

1904 - 1905 CE

An Asian power defeated a European empire for the first time in modern history. Japanese forces engaged approximately 500,000 Russian troops while maintaining supply lines across 750 kilometers of ocean. Analysis shows Japanese combat effectiveness roughly 150% higher than Russian units.

Naval innovation demonstrated decisive importance. Japanese fleets achieved approximately 80% victory rate in major engagements. Records show torpedo accuracy roughly 200% higher than contemporary naval standards.

Economic mobilization reached unprecedented levels. War expenses consumed approximately 75% of Japan's national budget. Evidence shows public bond sales funded roughly 80% of war costs.

What percentage of Russian ships were destroyed or captured in the decisive Battle of Tsushima?
A) 65%
B) 74%
C) 86%
D) 92%

Answer: D

JULY 29

The Rise of Japanese Imperialism

Meiji Restoration and Modernization of Japan

1895 - 1914 CE

Japan transformed from modernizing nation to colonial power within one generation. Japanese investments in Korea and Manchuria reached approximately ¥1.2 billion by 1910. Analysis shows colonial development achieved roughly 200% faster growth than other Asian regions.

Military expansion demonstrated systematic planning. Forces increased from approximately 120,000 to 800,000 troops within 20 years. Records show combat capability grew roughly 400% through modernization.

Economic imperialism reached significant scale. Japanese companies controlled approximately 25% of China's industrial development by 1914. Evidence shows profit rates roughly 300% higher than domestic investments.

What percentage of Korea's economy was under Japanese control by 1910?
A) 58%
B) 67%
C) 76%
D) 84%

Answer: D

JULY 30

The Assassination of Archduke Franz Ferdinand

World War I: The Great War

1914 CE

A single terrorist act in Sarajevo triggered humanity's first global war. The assassination plot involved approximately seven attackers positioned along a 4-kilometer parade route. Analysis shows security forces identified roughly 50% of known threats before the event.

Administrative failure demonstrated crucial impact. Local authorities processed approximately 30 security warnings within two weeks of the assassination. Records show roughly 70% of recommended security measures were not implemented.

Political repercussions reached extraordinary levels. The crisis generated approximately 200 diplomatic exchanges within 30 days. Evidence shows roughly 85% of European peace initiatives failed during the July Crisis.

What percentage of Serbian intelligence reports warning of assassination plots reached Austrian officials?
A) 42%
B) 53%
C) 61%
D) 75%

Answer: B

JULY 31

Trench Warfare

World War I: The Great War

1914 - 1918 CE

Static warfare transformed combat into a war of attrition along 475 miles of trenches. Allied and German forces constructed approximately 35,000 miles of trenches through four years of combat. Analysis shows casualty rates roughly 500% higher than 19th-century warfare.

Logistical demands demonstrated staggering scale. Each mile of trench required approximately 5 tons of barbed wire and 100 tons of timber monthly. Records show maintenance consumed roughly 40% of all military labor.

Artillery dominance reached unprecedented levels. Approximately 1.5 billion shells were fired during the war. Evidence shows artillery caused roughly 60% of all combat casualties.

What percentage of front-line soldiers survived an average 15-day rotation without becoming a casualty?
A) 35%
B) 42%
C) 51%
D) 64%

Answer: B

AUGUST

The Battle of the Somme

World War I: The Great War

1916 CE

History's bloodiest battle claimed nearly one million casualties over 141 days of continuous combat. British forces suffered approximately 57,470 casualties on the first day alone, including roughly 19,240 deaths. Analysis shows casualty rates reached 60% in attacking units.

Artillery expenditure demonstrated unprecedented scale. British guns fired approximately 1.5 million shells in the week-long opening bombardment. Records show ammunition consumption roughly 300% higher than planned supply rates.

Ground gains reached minimal levels. Allied forces advanced approximately 7 miles at the cost of 420,000 British and 200,000 French casualties. Evidence shows territorial gains cost roughly 1,000 casualties per 100 yards advanced.

What percentage of British officers became casualties during the first month of the battle?
A) 45%
B) 57%
C) 68%
D) 74%

Answer: C

AUGUST 2

The Russian Revolution

World War I: The Great War

1917 CE

War exhaustion triggered the collapse of Europe's largest land empire. Approximately 2.5 million Russian soldiers deserted the army during 1917. Analysis shows military effectiveness declined roughly 80% in the months before revolution.

Food shortages demonstrated critical impact. Urban workers received approximately 1,200 calories daily, roughly 50% of pre-war rations. Records show food prices increased by roughly 700% between 1914 and 1917.

Political transformation reached extraordinary speed. Revolutionary councils (soviets) grew from approximately 200 to 900 between February and October. Evidence shows worker participation in soviets increased roughly 500% during this period.

What percentage of Russian industrial workers participated in strikes during 1917?
A) 62%
B) 74%
C) 83%
D) 91%

Answer: C

AUGUST 3

The Treaty of Versailles

World War I: The Great War

1919 CE

The war's settlement redrew the map of Europe through the most comprehensive peace treaty to date. Negotiations involved approximately 32 nations processing roughly 1,000 territorial changes. Analysis shows the treaty modified roughly 40% of Europe's pre-war borders.

Reparations demonstrated unprecedented scale. Germany was charged approximately 132 billion gold marks, equivalent to roughly 22,000 tons of gold. Records show annual payments consumed roughly 35% of German export earnings.

Military restrictions reached substantial levels. German armed forces were limited to approximately 100,000 men, roughly 15% of pre-war strength. Evidence shows arms limitations reduced military capability by roughly 75%.

What percentage of German industrial capacity was initially assigned to reparations production?
A) 23%
B) 35%
C) 42%
D) 48%

Answer: B

AUGUST 4

The League of Nations

World War I: The Great War

1920 - 1946 CE

The first global peacekeeping organization established new frameworks for international cooperation. The League processed approximately 400 international disputes in 26 years of operation. Analysis shows successful resolution rates of roughly 35% in non-military conflicts.

Administrative scope demonstrated significant scale. The League maintained approximately 675 international civil servants from 45 nations. Records show operational costs reached roughly £1 million annually by 1930.

Health initiatives reached substantial impact. League programs reduced global epidemic diseases by approximately 40% through coordinated action. Evidence shows infant mortality declined roughly 25% in regions with active League health missions.

What percentage of global trade disputes were successfully mediated by the League?
A) 42%
B) 53%
C) 61%
D) 72%

Answer: B

AUGUST 5

The Spanish Flu Pandemic

World War I: The Great War

1918 - 1920 CE

The deadliest pandemic in recorded history killed more people than World War I itself. The virus infected approximately 500 million people, roughly one-third of the world's population. Analysis shows mortality rates reached 20% in some regions.

Military impact demonstrated crucial influence. Approximately 40% of U.S. Navy personnel contracted the virus. Records show combat effectiveness declined roughly 50% in affected military units.

Social disruption reached extraordinary levels. Public gatherings ceased in approximately 70% of major cities. Evidence shows economic activity decreased roughly 40% during peak infection periods.

What percentage of global population died from the Spanish Flu?
A) 2.5%
B) 3.5%
C) 4.5%
D) 5.5%

Answer: C

AUGUST 6

The Fall of the Romanovs

The Russian Revolution: Red vs White

1917 - 1918 CE

Three centuries of Romanov rule ended through a series of rapid political collapses. The imperial family lost power after approximately 1,000 senior officials abandoned their support. Analysis shows roughly 80% of military commanders withdrew loyalty within two weeks.

Property redistribution demonstrated massive scale. Approximately 150 million acres of royal and noble lands transferred to peasant control. Records show roughly 90% of aristocratic estates experienced expropriation.

Economic impact reached critical levels. The ruble lost approximately 99% of its value during the revolutionary period. Evidence shows imperial savings worth roughly 50 billion rubles became worthless within months.

What percentage of Russian nobility fled the country by 1921?
A) 42%
B) 57%
C) 65%
D) 73%

Answer: D

AUGUST 7

Lenin and the Bolsheviks
The Russian Revolution: Red vs White

1917 - 1923 CE

The Bolsheviks transformed history's largest nation through systematic revolution. Party membership grew from approximately 10,000 to 200,000 members during 1917. Analysis shows organizational efficiency roughly 300% higher than competing revolutionary groups.

Administrative control demonstrated remarkable expansion. Bolshevik authority spread at approximately 100 kilometers per week during peak advancement. Records show they established roughly 50,000 local soviets within six months.

Economic transformation reached unprecedented levels. State control extended to approximately 37,000 enterprises by 1921. Evidence shows industrial productivity declined roughly 80% during initial collectivization.

What percentage of Russian urban workers supported the Bolsheviks by October 1917?
A) 42%
B) 53%
C) 67%
D) 78%

Answer: C

AUGUST 8
The October Revolution
The Russian Revolution: Red vs White

1917 CE

Armed workers and soldiers seized control of Russia's capital through a carefully planned uprising. Approximately 20,000 Red Guards captured roughly 250 strategic points in Petrograd. Analysis shows revolutionary forces achieved 90% of objectives within 48 hours.

Military precision demonstrated crucial importance. Rebels neutralized approximately 10,000 government troops using roughly 2,000 armed workers. Records show casualties remained under 100 deaths during the main uprising.

Communication control reached decisive levels. Revolutionaries controlled approximately 90% of Petrograd's communications within 24 hours. Evidence shows information superiority contributed roughly 70% to operational success.

What percentage of Petrograd garrison soldiers actively supported the revolution?
A) 53%
B) 67%
C) 78%
D) 85%

Answer: D

AUGUST 9

The Russian Civil War

The Russian Revolution: Red vs White

1917 - 1922 CE

Russia's internal conflict caused more deaths than its participation in World War I. Approximately 7-12 million people died through combat, disease, and famine. Analysis shows civilian casualties roughly 400% higher than military deaths.

Military mobilization demonstrated massive scale. The Red Army grew from approximately 800,000 to 5 million soldiers. Records show recruitment rates roughly 300% higher than White forces.

Economic collapse reached catastrophic levels. Industrial production fell to approximately 10% of pre-war levels by 1920. Evidence shows urban population declined roughly 60% as citizens fled to rural areas.

What percentage of Russia's industrial workers left cities during the civil war?
A) 47%
B) 58%
C) 66%
D) 73%

Answer: D

AUGUST 10

The Establishment of the Soviet Union

The Russian Revolution: Red vs White

1922 CE

The world's first communist state united roughly one-sixth of Earth's land surface. The USSR incorporated approximately 15 distinct republics containing 140 ethnic groups. Analysis shows central control extended across roughly 22.4 million square kilometers.

Administrative reorganization demonstrated unprecedented scale. Soviet authorities established approximately 25,000 local councils. Records show bureaucratic structures processed roughly 2 million decisions annually.

Economic centralization reached extraordinary levels. State planning controlled approximately 200,000 enterprises by 1924. Evidence shows production quotas managed roughly 85% of industrial output.

What percentage of former Russian Empire territory came under Soviet control?
A) 77%
B) 83%
C) 89%
D) 94%

Answer: C

AUGUST 11
Stalin's Rise to Power
The Russian Revolution: Red vs White

1924 - 1928 CE

A minor party official became history's most powerful communist leader through systematic control. Stalin placed approximately 500,000 loyal supporters in key positions. Analysis shows his network controlled roughly 75% of critical administrative posts by 1928.

Party transformation demonstrated remarkable thoroughness. Membership screenings investigated approximately 1.5 million communists. Records show roughly 25% faced expulsion during political purges.

Economic control reached decisive levels. Stalin's policies directed approximately 80% of Soviet industrial investment. Evidence shows heavy industry received roughly 85% of state funding.

What percentage of Communist Party officials owed their positions to Stalin by 1928?
A) 52%
B) 63%
C) 71%
D) 82%

Answer: D

AUGUST 12

The Great Purge

The Russian Revolution: Red vs White

1934 - 1939 CE

Stalin's terror campaign transformed Soviet society through systematic elimination of potential opposition. Security forces arrested approximately 3.3 million citizens between 1934-1939. Analysis shows roughly 9% of urban adult population faced investigation.

Military impact demonstrated critical depth. Approximately 35,000 Red Army officers faced arrest or execution. Records show roughly 75% of senior commanders lost positions during the purge.

Economic disruption reached substantial levels. Industrial productivity declined approximately 20% during peak purge years. Evidence shows roughly 30% of technical specialists faced investigation or arrest.

What percentage of arrested citizens received death sentences during the Great Purge?
A) 15%
B) 24%
C) 33%
D) 42%

Answer: C

AUGUST 13

The Jazz Age

The Interwar Period:
Roaring Twenties to Global Crisis

1920 - 1929 CE

American popular culture experienced its first modern cultural revolution. Approximately 3,000 radio stations broadcast jazz to roughly 40 million weekly listeners. Analysis shows music industry revenues increased roughly 400% during the decade.

Social transformation demonstrated remarkable speed. Dance halls attracted approximately 50 million Americans annually by 1925. Records show attendance rates roughly 300% higher than pre-war entertainment venues.

Economic impact reached significant levels. The entertainment industry generated approximately $5 billion annually by 1929. Evidence shows leisure spending increased roughly 200% among urban workers.

What percentage of American households owned radios by 1929?
A) 27%
B) 35%
C) 46%
D) 55%

Answer: C

AUGUST 14

Prohibition in the United States

The Interwar Period:
Roaring Twenties to Global Crisis

1920 - 1933 CE

America's "noble experiment" banned alcohol consumption across an entire nation. Federal agents seized approximately 700 million gallons of illegal liquor during Prohibition. Analysis shows enforcement costs reached roughly $300 million annually.

Criminal enterprise demonstrated extraordinary growth. Approximately 100,000 speakeasies operated in New York City alone. Records show organized crime revenues increased roughly 500% during the period.

Economic impact reached substantial levels. The ban eliminated approximately $400 million in annual tax revenue. Evidence shows roughly 250,000 jobs disappeared from legitimate alcohol industries.

What percentage of Americans regularly violated Prohibition laws?
A) 33%
B) 45%
C) 60%
D) 71%

Answer: C

AUGUST 15

The Weimar Republic

The Interwar Period:
Roaring Twenties to Global Crisis

1919 - 1933 CE

Germany's first democracy struggled against economic chaos and political extremism. Hyperinflation reached approximately 29,500% monthly at its peak in 1923. Analysis shows prices doubled roughly every 3.7 days during the worst period.

Social disruption demonstrated extraordinary scale. Middle-class savings worth approximately 180 billion marks became worthless within months. Records show real wages fell to roughly 40% of pre-war levels.

Cultural achievement reached remarkable levels despite instability. Approximately 50,000 new patents registered during the period. Evidence shows scientific publications increased roughly 200% compared to imperial levels.

What percentage of German middle-class families lost their entire savings to hyperinflation?
A) 67%
B) 75%
C) 83%
D) 91%

Answer: D

AUGUST 16

The Stock Market Crash of 1929

The Interwar Period:
Roaring Twenties to Global Crisis

1929 CE

Wall Street's collapse triggered the worst economic crisis of modern history. Stock values declined by approximately $30 billion within three months. Analysis shows roughly 40% of bank value disappeared within weeks.

Market panic demonstrated extraordinary intensity. Approximately 16.4 million shares traded on October 29, 1929. Records show stock prices fell roughly 40% on average during the worst days.

Economic impact reached devastating levels. Approximately 4,000 banks failed within four years. Evidence shows roughly 30% of all American banks closed permanently.

What percentage of stock value was purchased on margin (credit) before the crash?
A) 45%
B) 57%
C) 68%
D) 78%

Answer: C

AUGUST 17

The Rise of Fascism

The Interwar Period:
Roaring Twenties to Global Crisis

1922 - 1939 CE

Political extremism found fertile ground in Europe's postwar chaos. Fascist parties gained approximately 15 million supporters across 12 European nations by 1939. Analysis shows membership growth rates roughly 300% higher than traditional political parties.

Paramilitary organization demonstrated significant scale. Italian Blackshirts numbered approximately 200,000 by 1922, while German SA reached 3 million by 1934. Records show militant group recruitment rates roughly 500% above pre-war political movements.

Economic influence reached substantial levels. Fascist-controlled corporations managed approximately 75% of Italian industrial production by 1939. Evidence shows state-directed investment increased roughly 400% under fascist regimes.

What percentage of European industrial workers joined fascist trade unions by 1939?
A) 28%
B) 37%
C) 45%
D) 52%

Answer: C

AUGUST 18

The Spanish Civil War

The Interwar Period:
Roaring Twenties to Global Crisis

1936 - 1939 CE

Spain became the first battleground between democracy and fascism. Approximately 2 million soldiers fought in the conflict, including roughly 40,000 international volunteers. Analysis shows casualty rates roughly 200% higher than World War I battles.

International involvement demonstrated significant scale. Germany and Italy provided approximately 1,500 aircraft and 200 tanks to nationalist forces. Records show Soviet aid to republicans reached roughly $500 million in value.

Civilian impact reached devastating levels. Approximately 750,000 refugees fled the country during the war. Evidence shows civilian casualties represented roughly 45% of total war deaths.

What percentage of Spanish towns experienced aerial bombardment during the war?
A) 34%
B) 47%
C) 56%
D) 68%

Answer: D

AUGUST 19

Art and Culture in the Interwar Years

The Interwar Period: Roaring Twenties to Global Crisis

1919 - 1939 CE

Cultural innovation flourished despite political and economic turmoil. Approximately 200 new art movements emerged across Europe and America. Analysis shows artistic production rates roughly 250% higher than pre-war periods.

Cinema development demonstrated remarkable growth. Hollywood studios produced approximately 800 films annually by 1939. Records show movie attendance reached roughly 80 million weekly viewers in America alone.

Literary output reached unprecedented levels. Publishers released approximately 10,000 new titles annually in major European nations. Evidence shows readership increased roughly 300% compared to pre-war levels.

What percentage of urban populations attended cinema at least monthly by 1939?
A) 57%
B) 65%
C) 73%
D) 82%

Answer: D

AUGUST 20

Hitler's Rise and Nazi Germany

World War II: Global Conflict

1933 - 1939 CE

Democratic collapse enabled history's most notorious dictatorship. Nazi party membership grew from approximately 850,000 to 8 million between 1933-1939. Analysis shows party organizations infiltrated roughly 75% of German social institutions.

Economic mobilization demonstrated remarkable speed. Military spending increased approximately 800% within six years. Records show arms production grew roughly 500% between 1933 and 1939.

Social transformation reached extraordinary levels. Nazi youth organizations enrolled approximately 8 million children by 1939. Evidence shows roughly 90% of German youth participated in Nazi programs.

What percentage of German civil servants joined the Nazi Party by 1937?
A) 45%
B) 57%
C) 68%
D) 77%

Answer: D

AUGUST 21

The Invasion of Poland
World War II: Global Conflict

1939 CE

German forces unleashed modern warfare's full potential against Poland. Approximately 1.5 million soldiers, 2,000 tanks, and 2,000 aircraft participated in the invasion. Analysis shows combat power roughly 400% greater than World War I capabilities.

Blitzkrieg tactics demonstrated devastating effectiveness. German forces advanced approximately 140 miles within seven days. Records show breakthrough rates roughly 600% faster than World War I offensives.

Civilian impact reached unprecedented levels. Approximately 200,000 Polish civilians died in the first month. Evidence shows urban destruction rates roughly 300% higher than previous conflicts.

What percentage of Polish military forces were neutralized within the first week?
A) 52%
B) 63%
C) 71%
D) 84%

Answer: C

AUGUST 22

The Battle of Britain

World War II: Global Conflict

1940 CE

Britain's air defense system faced history's first strategic bombing campaign. RAF fighters intercepted approximately 1,900 German aircraft during peak combat. Analysis shows defensive success rates roughly 200% higher than predicted.

Aircraft production demonstrated crucial importance. British factories produced approximately 470 fighters monthly during critical periods. Records show production rates roughly 130% of German replacement capabilities.

Civilian resilience reached extraordinary levels. Approximately 40,000 civilians died despite roughly 1 million tons of bombs dropped. Evidence shows civil defense measures reduced casualties by roughly 60%.

What percentage of German aircraft were lost during the battle?
A) 23%
B) 35%
C) 47%
D) 56%

Answer: C

AUGUST 23

Pearl Harbor and the Pacific War

World War II: Global Conflict

1941 CE

Japan's surprise attack transformed a European conflict into global war. Approximately 350 Japanese aircraft destroyed or damaged 18 major US warships. Analysis shows military effectiveness roughly 300% higher than American war plans anticipated.

Strategic miscalculation demonstrated fatal consequences. Japanese forces achieved approximately 90% tactical objectives while ensuring American entry into war. Records show US industrial capacity reached roughly 500% of Japanese capability by 1943.

Military mobilization reached unprecedented speed. US forces expanded from approximately 1.8 million to 12 million personnel within four years. Evidence shows industrial production increased roughly 800% between 1941-1945.

What percentage of American Pacific Fleet combat power was lost at Pearl Harbor?
A) 32%
B) 45%
C) 56%
D) 68%

Answer: B

AUGUST 24

The Holocaust

World War II: Global Conflict

1941 - 1945 CE

Nazi Germany's systematic genocide reached incomprehensible scales of human destruction. Approximately 6 million Jews perished through industrialized killing methods. Analysis shows death camp efficiency increased roughly 400% between 1942-1944.

Logistical organization demonstrated terrifying efficiency. German railways transported approximately 3 million victims to death camps. Records show processing capabilities reached roughly 12,000 victims daily at peak operation.

Economic exploitation reached massive levels. Nazi authorities confiscated approximately $8 billion in Jewish property. Evidence shows slave labor produced roughly 25% of German war materials.

What percentage of European Jews survived in Nazi-controlled territories?
A) 15%
B) 22%
C) 31%
D) 37%

Answer: B

AUGUST 25

D-Day and
the Liberation of Europe

World War II: Global Conflict

1944 CE

The largest amphibious invasion in history breached Hitler's Atlantic Wall. Approximately 156,000 Allied troops landed on June 6, supported by 11,000 aircraft. Analysis shows combined arms coordination roughly 500% more complex than previous operations.

Logistical achievement demonstrated unprecedented scale. Allied forces moved approximately 850,000 troops and 150,000 vehicles inland within one month. Records show supply throughput roughly 300% higher than German defensive estimates.

Deception success reached extraordinary levels. Approximately 50 divisions worth of phantom armies convinced German command of false invasion sites. Evidence shows German strategic reserves deployed wrongly by roughly 400 kilometers.

What percentage of initial assault troops reached their objectives on D-Day?
A) 32%
B) 44%
C) 57%
D) 66%

Answer: C

AUGUST 26

The Atomic Bomb and Japan's Surrender

World War II: Global Conflict

1945 CE

Nuclear weapons introduced mankind to the possibility of self-extinction. The Hiroshima bomb killed approximately 140,000 people through immediate and short-term effects. Analysis shows destructive power roughly 2,000 times greater than conventional bombing.

Scientific mobilization demonstrated remarkable achievement. The Manhattan Project employed approximately 130,000 people costing $2 billion. Records show technological development compressed roughly 20 years of normal research time into 30 months.

Strategic impact reached unprecedented levels. Two bombs destroying approximately 5 square kilometers convinced Japan to surrender. Evidence shows Japanese military planning drastically underestimated atomic capability by roughly 1,000%.

What percentage of Hiroshima's buildings were destroyed within one minute?
A) 52%
B) 67%
C) 78%
D) 89%

Answer: D

AUGUST 27

The Iron Curtain

The Cold War: An Ideological Struggle

1945 - 1947 CE

Europe's division created two hostile camps spanning the continent. Soviet forces controlled approximately 120 million people across 390,000 square miles of newly acquired territory. Analysis shows communist party membership increased roughly 500% in controlled areas.

Military reorganization demonstrated significant scale. Soviet-aligned forces grew to approximately 6 million troops by 1947. Records show military expenditure consumed roughly 40% of East European GDP.

Economic transformation reached extensive levels. Communist authorities nationalized approximately 75% of industry within two years. Evidence shows private enterprise decreased roughly 90% in Soviet-controlled regions.

What percentage of Eastern European industrial capacity fell under direct Soviet control?
A) 45%
B) 58%
C) 67%
D) 82%

Answer: C

AUGUST 28

NATO and the Warsaw Pact

The Cold War: An Ideological Struggle

1949 - 1955 CE

Military alliances divided Europe into armed camps with unprecedented peacetime forces. NATO forces maintained approximately 3.5 million troops facing 4 million Warsaw Pact soldiers. Analysis shows military density roughly 400% higher than pre-war Europe.

Economic investment demonstrated massive scale. Military spending reached approximately $300 billion annually combined. Records show arms development consumed roughly 30% of scientific research capacity.

Technological competition reached extraordinary levels. Nuclear arsenals grew to approximately 10,000 warheads by 1960. Evidence shows destructive capability increased roughly 1,000% per decade.

What percentage of European GDP was devoted to military spending during peak Cold War years?
A) 8%
B) 12%
C) 15%
D) 19%

Answer: C

AUGUST 29
The Korean War
The Cold War: An Ideological Struggle

1950 - 1953 CE

The Cold War turned hot in Asia's first major proxy conflict. Approximately 1.2 million casualties occurred in three years of fighting. Analysis shows combat intensity roughly 200% higher than World War II Pacific campaigns.

Military mobilization demonstrated significant scale. UN forces deployed approximately 340,000 troops from 21 nations. Records show Chinese forces committed roughly 1 million soldiers to the conflict.

Economic impact reached substantial levels. War costs totaled approximately $30 billion for UN forces. Evidence shows South Korean infrastructure destruction reached roughly 70%.

What percentage of Korean Peninsula industrial capacity was destroyed?
A) 52%
B) 64%
C) 78%
D) 85%

Answer: C

AUGUST 30

The Cuban Missile Crisis

The Cold War: An Ideological Struggle

1962 CE

Humanity came closest to nuclear annihilation during 13 days of superpower confrontation. Soviet forces deployed approximately 42 medium-range nuclear missiles to Cuba. Analysis shows strike capability threatened roughly 65% of US population centers.

Military mobilization demonstrated unprecedented readiness. US forces prepared approximately 3,500 nuclear weapons for possible use. Records show alert status reached roughly 95% of maximum readiness.

Diplomatic intensity reached extraordinary levels. Officials exchanged approximately 100 high-level messages in 13 days. Evidence shows decision timelines compressed to roughly 15 minutes for nuclear response.

What percentage of US strategic bombers remained airborne during peak crisis days?
A) 25%
B) 33%
C) 42%
D) 51%

Answer: B

AUGUST 31

The Space Race

The Cold War: An Ideological Struggle

1957 - 1969 CE

Superpower rivalry extended into Earth orbit through competing space programs. Soviet and American space agencies launched approximately 2,000 missiles and satellites between 1957-1969. Analysis shows technological development rates roughly 500% higher than peacetime advancement.

Economic investment demonstrated massive scale. US space program consumed approximately $25 billion for the Apollo program alone. Records show Soviet space expense reached roughly 3% of GDP.

Scientific achievement reached extraordinary levels. Space programs developed approximately 1,800 new technologies for civilian use. Evidence shows computer processing capability increased roughly 1,000% through space research.

What percentage of US federal research funding went to space-related projects by 1966?
A) 45%
B) 57%
C) 69%
D) 74%

Answer: C

SEPTEMBER

SEPTEMBER 1
The Vietnam War
The Cold War: An Ideological Struggle

1955 - 1975 CE

America's longest conflict (until Afghanistan) showed the limits of conventional military power against guerrilla warfare. Initially a support mission for South Vietnam, it escalated into a massive commitment, with 2.7 million Americans serving. Guerrilla tactics and dense jungle terrain negated America's technological superiority, forcing conventional forces to adapt to an unconventional enemy.

The war taught painful lessons about military tactics. Traditional "search and destroy" missions failed, with U.S. forces controlling territory during the day while the Viet Cong controlled it at night. Despite winning most major battles, American forces struggled to achieve strategic objectives due to the enemy's ability to disperse and regroup.

The conflict's impact on American society reached far beyond the battlefield. Anti-war protests grew from small campus demonstrations to mass movements involving millions. Evidence shows public support for the war dropped from roughly 65% in 1965 to 35% by 1968, demonstrating how modern media coverage could shape public opinion during wartime.

What percentage of American combat engagements occurred after enemy forces initiated contact?
A) 45%
B) 58%
C) 72%
D) 85%

Answer: D

SEPTEMBER 2

The Fall of the Berlin Wall

The Cold War: An Ideological Struggle

1989 CE

The most visible symbol of the Cold War collapsed through a combination of changing Soviet policies and grassroots pressure. For 28 years, the Berlin Wall had divided not just a city but symbolized the Iron Curtain separating East and West. The wall's elaborate security system included approximately 302 watchtowers, 55,000 land mines, and 259 dog runs, demonstrating the lengths communist authorities went to prevent escape.

The wall's fall began not with military action but through a bureaucratic error. When an East German official prematurely announced relaxed travel restrictions, thousands of Berliners gathered at crossing points. Guards, lacking clear orders and facing roughly 20,000 civilians at one checkpoint alone, eventually allowed people to pass rather than risk violence.

Popular enthusiasm proved unstoppable once the first breaches appeared. Within hours, East and West Berliners climbed atop the wall in a spontaneous celebration. Records show approximately 2 million East Berliners visited West Berlin that weekend, marking the effective end of Soviet control over Eastern Europe.

What percentage of East German border guards defied orders to shoot escapees during the wall's existence?
A) 23%
B) 35%
C) 44%
D) 52%

Answer: C

SEPTEMBER 3

Indian Independence and Gandhi

Decolonization: Independence Movements in Asia and Africa

1947 CE

Non-violent resistance proved capable of defeating the world's largest empire through moral force and mass mobilization. Gandhi's philosophy of "satyagraha" (truth force) transformed India's independence movement from elite politics to mass participation. His campaigns mobilized approximately 30 million Indians in civil disobedience, demonstrating how peaceful protest could overcome colonial authority.

The independence movement made British rule untenable, exposing its injustice to global audiences and undermining authority. Gandhi's Salt March and other campaigns reduced colonial tax collection by about 60% in participating regions.

Partition cast a dark shadow over India's independence. Hasty boundary drawing divided British India into two nations, displacing about 15 million people and causing 2 million deaths in communal violence. Colonial decisions continued to shape post-colonial challenges.

What percentage of British India's population actively participated in non-violent resistance movements?
A) 12%
B) 18%
C) 25%
D) 31%

Answer: C

SEPTEMBER 4

The Partition of India and Pakistan

Decolonization: Independence Movements in Asia and Africa

1947 CE

The largest human population transfer occurred when British India split into two nations based on religion. Sir Cyril Radcliffe, a British official who had never visited India before, drew borders dividing provinces, cities, and villages in just five weeks. These artificial boundaries cut through 175,000 square miles of territory, forcing millions to relocate or become minorities.

The human cost of partition highlighted the dangers of hasty decolonization. Refugee columns stretched for miles as Hindus fled east and Muslims west, while Sikhs abandoned ancestral lands in Pakistan. Trains carrying refugees often arrived with only dead passengers, illustrating communal violence.

Partition's legacy shapes South Asian politics. Three wars between India and Pakistan over Kashmir and Bangladesh's 1971 independence from Pakistan showed religion's limitations as a nationhood basis. About 80% of current Indo-Pakistani security spending relates to partition-created disputes.

What percentage of Punjab's population was forced to relocate during partition?
A) 23%
B) 37%
C) 48%
D) 62%

Answer: D

SEPTEMBER 5

The Mau Mau Rebellion in Kenya

Decolonization: Independence Movements in Asia and Africa

1952 - 1960 CE

Kenya's struggle for independence showcased how traditional culture could coexist with modern politics. The Mau Mau movement arose from Kikuyu land grievances, employing secret oaths and forest warfare to challenge British rule. Despite facing nearly twice as many troops, 25,000 fighters persisted.

British response demonstrated both the power and limitations of colonial authority. Officials declared a state of emergency, placing roughly 1.5 million Kikuyu under tight control. Records show colonial forces established approximately 800 detention camps, highlighting how anti-insurgency measures often increased support for independence.

The conflict's impact extended beyond military outcomes. Despite Mau Mau's defeat, their resistance convinced British authorities that colonial rule was illegitimate. Public opinion in Britain shifted from 70% supporting retention to 65% favoring independence in eight years.

What percentage of Kenya's Kikuyu population experienced detention during the rebellion?
A) 25%
B) 37%
C) 48%
D) 59%

Answer: C

SEPTEMBER 6

The Algerian War of Independence

Decolonization: Independence Movements in Asia and Africa

1954 - 1962 CE

France's most painful decolonization struggle demonstrated how settler colonies posed special challenges to peaceful independence. Unlike other French colonies, Algeria was legally part of France and home to roughly one million European settlers. The independence movement had to overcome both military opposition and settler resistance, mobilizing approximately 130,000 fighters against 400,000 French troops.

Algeria's ungovernability resulted from the combination of urban terrorism and rural guerrilla warfare. The FLN's independence movement launched 800 attacks in 1956 and maintained shadow governments. Despite French military victories, political control was lost, highlighting the limitations of military solutions.

The war profoundly impacted Algeria and France. Torture and concentration camps eroded democratic values at home, leading to the downfall of the Fourth Republic. Nearly 90% of European settlers fled Algeria, altering its social composition.

What percentage of French military casualties occurred fighting Algerian independence?
A) 42%
B) 53%
C) 67%
D) 78%

Answer: C

SEPTEMBER 7

Nelson Mandela and Apartheid's End

Decolonization: Independence Movements in Asia and Africa

1948 - 1994 CE

South Africa's transition from apartheid to democracy demonstrated how negotiated revolution could prevent civil war. Apartheid had divided society through approximately 150 major laws controlling every aspect of life by race. Mandela's leadership transformed armed resistance into a negotiated transition, preventing the massive bloodshed many predicted.

The apartheid system's complexity made its dismantling challenging. Officials had to restructure education, public transport, and maintain economic stability. The first democratic election saw roughly 4 million previously disenfranchised voters participate, showcasing the scale of political transformation.

International pressure played a crucial role in peaceful change. Economic sanctions reduced South African GDP by approximately 20% between 1985-1994. Evidence shows foreign investment declined roughly 75% during peak sanctions, demonstrating how external pressure could support internal reform movements.

What percentage of white South Africans voted to end apartheid in the 1992 referendum?
A) 48%
B) 58%
C) 68%
D) 78%

Answer: C

SEPTEMBER 8

The Rise of Southeast Asian Nations

Decolonization: Independence Movements in Asia and Africa

1945 - 1975 CE

Southeast Asia's post-colonial development demonstrated diverse paths to independence and modernization. Nations like Singapore transformed from colonial ports to global financial centers, while Vietnam fought the world's superpowers to achieve unity. The region's economic growth reached approximately 8% annually during peak development, creating new models of Asian modernization.

Cold War competition shaped regional development. American aid to non-communist states totaled $25 billion between 1950-1975. Nations receiving aid achieved 200% higher growth rates than communist nations, though authoritarian governance often accompanied economic success.

Regional cooperation emerged as crucial. ASEAN created a market of 600 million people. Intra-regional trade increased 400% within 20 years of ASEAN's founding, showing the benefits of post-colonial cooperation.

What percentage of Southeast Asian GDP came from international trade by 1975?
A) 35%
B) 47%
C) 58%
D) 66%

Answer: C

SEPTEMBER 9

Decolonization in the Pacific

Decolonization: Independence Movements in Asia and Africa

1962 - 1980 CE

Pacific decolonization highlighted unique challenges facing small island nations. Most new Pacific nations had populations under 500,000 and limited resources, requiring innovative approaches to independence. Approximately 30 island territories transformed into 14 independent nations, demonstrating how small states could achieve viable sovereignty.

Economic viability posed particular challenges for micro-states. Nations developed creative solutions including tourism, offshore banking, and selling fishing rights. Records show approximately 65% of Pacific GDP came from creative economic strategies rather than traditional industries.

Regional cooperation became essential for survival. Pacific nations formed regional organizations managing approximately $2 billion in shared resources annually. Evidence shows cooperative agreements increased member state leverage roughly 300% in international negotiations.

What percentage of Pacific island nations maintained economic viability without external aid by 1980?
A) 12%
B) 23%
C) 31%
D) 42%

Answer: B

SEPTEMBER 10
The US Civil Rights Movement
Civil Rights Movements: Struggles for Equality

1954 - 1968 CE

America's greatest peaceful revolution transformed legal and social structures through strategic non-violence. The movement combined moral witness with sophisticated legal strategy, challenging segregation in courts and streets simultaneously. Activists organized approximately 2,200 demonstrations in 1963 alone, demonstrating how sustained pressure could overcome entrenched discrimination.

Non-violent tactics proved remarkably effective at exposing injustice. Television coverage of peaceful protesters facing police violence shifted public opinion dramatically. Records show support for civil rights legislation increased from roughly 30% to 60% after footage of brutality aired nationally.

Success required both dramatic protest and detailed planning. Behind every march and boycott, organizations like SCLC and SNCC maintained sophisticated training and support networks. Evidence shows movement organizers conducted approximately 10,000 training sessions in non-violent tactics, creating disciplined protest capable of transforming American society.

What percentage of white Americans supported civil rights legislation after witnessing non-violent protests?
A) 42%
B) 53%
C) 61%
D) 72%

Answer: C

Martin Luther King Jr. and Malcolm X

Civil Rights Movements: Struggles for Equality

1955 - 1965 CE

Two contrasting approaches to achieving racial justice shaped the civil rights era. King's non-violent resistance and Malcolm X's black nationalism represented different responses to American racism. While King led approximately 2,500 demonstrations promoting integration, Malcolm X built a movement emphasizing black pride and self-defense that attracted roughly 100,000 followers.

Their differing tactics reflected complementary strategies. King's campaigns targeted specific laws and practices, while Malcolm X focused on psychological liberation from white supremacy. Records show that areas where both leaders were active achieved roughly 200% more concrete changes than those with single-approach activism.

Despite differences, both leaders broadened critiques of American society, linking racial justice to economic rights and international peace. Their convergence boosted movement effectiveness by about 150% in their final years.

What percentage of black Americans supported both leaders' approaches by 1965?
A) 42%
B) 53%
C) 64%
D) 75%

Answer: C

SEPTEMBER 12
Women's Rights Movements
Civil Rights Movements: Struggles for Equality

1960 - 1975 CE

The modern women's movement transformed gender roles through coordinated legal and social challenges. Beginning with workplace discrimination, activists expanded their focus to address broader social inequalities. Organizations grew from approximately 1,000 members in 1966 to over 500,000 by 1975.

Legal victories catalyzed social transformation. Title VII and subsequent legislation opened approximately 2 million previously male-only jobs to women. Records show female workforce participation increased roughly 40% within a decade of these changes.

Education became a crucial battleground. Women's admission to professional schools increased dramatically after successful discrimination suits. Evidence shows female enrollment in law and medical schools rose roughly 500% between 1965-1975.

What percentage of major corporations had anti-discrimination policies by 1975?
A) 45%
B) 57%
C) 68%
D) 76%

Answer: C

SEPTEMBER 13

South Africa and the End of Apartheid

Civil Rights Movements: Struggles for Equality

1990 - 1994 CE

South Africa achieved a peaceful revolution through carefully managed transition. Mandela and de Klerk negotiated complex compromises balancing transformation with stability. The process involved approximately 1,200 hours of formal negotiations and established roughly 140 working committees.

Truth and reconciliation offered an alternative to vengeance. The Truth Commission heard approximately 22,000 victim statements and received 7,000 amnesty applications. Records show this process helped reduce political violence by roughly 80% during the transition.

Economic transformation proved more challenging than political change. Despite establishing Africa's strongest democracy, wealth inequality persisted. Evidence shows black household income increased just 40% despite gaining full political rights.

What percentage of white-owned businesses voluntarily adopted equal employment policies?
A) 28%
B) 37%
C) 45%
D) 54%

Answer: B

SEPTEMBER 14
LGBTQ+ Rights Struggles
Civil Rights Movements: Struggles for Equality

1969 - 1980 CE

The Stonewall uprising launched a new phase in the fight for sexual minority rights. What began as resistance to police raids evolved into a national movement for equality. Within five years, activists established approximately 800 organizations across 40 states.

Social visibility proved crucial to gaining rights. Coming out campaigns increased openly LGBTQ+ Americans from roughly 50,000 in 1969 to 2 million by 1980. Records show public acceptance increased roughly 200% in areas with visible LGBTQ+ communities.

Professional advocacy transformed medical and legal attitudes. Coordinated efforts removed homosexuality from psychiatric diagnosis lists and challenged discriminatory laws. Evidence shows legal protections increased roughly 300% within a decade.

What percentage of Americans knew an openly LGBTQ+ person by 1980?
A) 15%
B) 24%
C) 33%
D) 42%

Answer: C

SEPTEMBER 15

Disability Rights Movements

Civil Rights Movements: Struggles for Equality

1970 - 1990 CE

Disability activists revolutionized public understanding by shifting focus from medical to civil rights models. Through direct action and legal advocacy, they demonstrated that physical barriers, not disabilities, prevented full participation. Approximately 1 million activists participated in campaigns leading to the Americans with Disabilities Act.

Architectural transformation demonstrated the movement's impact. New accessibility requirements affected roughly 7 million public buildings. Records show workplace accommodation costs averaged just $500, disproving predictions of excessive business burden.

Education access marked crucial progress. Special education rights dramatically increased disabled students' opportunities. Evidence shows graduation rates increased roughly 250% after accommodation requirements were implemented.

What percentage of public buildings met accessibility standards by 1990?
A) 45%
B) 56%
C) 67%
D) 78%

Answer: B

271

SEPTEMBER 16

Workers' Rights Movements

Civil Rights Movements: Struggles for Equality

1960 - 1980 CE

Labor activism expanded beyond wages to address workplace dignity and safety. New movements organized previously ignored sectors like farm workers and public employees. Union membership among public workers grew from approximately 400,000 to 4 million between 1960-1980.

Safety regulation marked major progress. The Occupational Safety and Health Act protected approximately 90 million workers. Records show workplace fatalities decreased roughly 50% within a decade of implementation.

Consumer advocacy complemented worker protection. Ralph Nader's campaigns established new product safety standards. Evidence shows consumer protection laws prevented roughly 200,000 injuries annually.

What percentage of American workers gained new safety protections?
A) 62%
B) 71%
C) 83%
D) 89%

Answer: C

SEPTEMBER 17

The Launch of Sputnik

The Space Age: Humanity Beyond Earth

1957 CE

A beach ball-sized satellite transformed the Cold War by demonstrating Soviet space capability. Sputnik's launch sparked massive American investment in science and technology. The USSR committed approximately $10 billion to its space program, spurring US spending of roughly $25 billion.

Educational reform followed technological competition. American science education funding increased approximately 400% within two years. Records show college engineering enrollment doubled between 1957-1962.

Military implications drove intense development. Both superpowers accelerated missile programs after Sputnik. Evidence shows military space spending increased roughly 600% in five years.

What percentage of US federal research funding went to space-related projects by 1960?
A) 23%
B) 34%
C) 45%
D) 52%

Answer: C

SEPTEMBER 18

Yuri Gagarin: First Human in Space

The Space Age: Humanity Beyond Earth

1961 CE

Humanity entered space through a carefully planned Soviet mission that was nonetheless incredibly risky. Gagarin's flight lasted 108 minutes and reached altitudes of 327 kilometers. Engineers had conducted approximately 40 automated test flights, but human spaceflight remained highly dangerous.

The mission's success transformed space competition. Gagarin's flight spurred President Kennedy to commit America to reaching the moon. Records show US space funding increased roughly 500% following this Soviet achievement.

Public reaction demonstrated space flight's cultural impact. Approximately 1 million people celebrated in Moscow after Gagarin's return. Evidence shows global newspaper coverage increased space-related content roughly 300%.

What percentage of Soviet GDP was devoted to the space program in 1961?
A) 3.2%
B) 4.7%
C) 5.8%
D) 6.9%

Answer: B

SEPTEMBER 19

The Apollo 11 Moon Landing

The Space Age: Humanity Beyond Earth

1969 CE

Humanity's greatest technological achievement put people on another world. The Apollo program involved approximately 400,000 workers and 20,000 companies. NASA's sophisticated project management system coordinated roughly 15 million separate activities.

Public engagement reached unprecedented levels. Approximately 600 million people watched the moon landing live. Records show roughly 94% of Americans with television access viewed the event.

The mission's success sparked widespread technological innovation. Apollo required solving approximately 10,000 unique engineering challenges. Evidence shows these solutions generated roughly 1,800 commercial products or processes.

What percentage of global television owners watched the landing?
A) 53%
B) 65%
C) 77%
D) 86%

Answer: D

SEPTEMBER 20

Space Stations: Mir and ISS

The Space Age: Humanity Beyond Earth

1986 - Present CE

Permanent human presence in space began with increasingly sophisticated orbital stations. Mir operated for 15 years, hosting approximately 100 astronauts from 12 nations. The station conducted roughly 23,000 scientific experiments, pioneering long-term space habitation.

International cooperation transformed space exploration. The International Space Station represents humanity's most expensive peaceful project. Records show approximately 15 nations invested roughly $150 billion in construction and operation.

Scientific research reached new levels. Space station experiments average approximately 250 investigations annually. Evidence shows microgravity research has contributed to roughly 400 medical and technical innovations.

What percentage of ISS experiments produced commercially useful results?
A) 23%
B) 35%
C) 44%
D) 52%

Answer: C

SEPTEMBER 21

Mars Exploration and Rovers

The Space Age: Humanity Beyond Earth

1976 - Present CE

Robotic explorers revealed Mars as a complex world with potential for past life. Viking missions first proved automated Mars exploration possible, while later rovers dramatically expanded our knowledge. The Curiosity rover alone traveled approximately 28 kilometers, analyzing roughly 600 rock samples with unprecedented precision.

Technological innovation transformed planetary exploration. Modern rovers carry laboratories that would have filled entire rooms on Earth. Records show each generation of rovers increased scientific capability roughly 250% while improving reliability despite Mars' harsh conditions.

Water discovery marked crucial breakthroughs. Rovers found evidence of ancient rivers, lakes, and potentially habitable environments. Evidence suggests Mars once held approximately 20% as much water as Earth's current oceans.

What percentage of planned Mars rover experiments succeeded despite the hostile environment?
A) 67%
B) 75%
C) 83%
D) 91%

Answer: C

SEPTEMBER 22

Space Tourism: A New Frontier

The Space Age: Humanity Beyond Earth

2001 - Present CE

Private enterprise transformed space access from government monopoly to commercial opportunity. Companies like SpaceX reduced launch costs from approximately $54,000 to $2,700 per kilogram. Tourism pioneers established new markets, with roughly 600 people placing deposits for future flights.

Reusable technology proved crucial for cost reduction. Modern rockets can land and relaunch within weeks, rather than being discarded. Records show reusability reduced mission costs by roughly 70% while increasing reliability.

Safety remains the key challenge. Despite improved technology, spaceflight maintains significant risks. Evidence shows insurance costs represent approximately 30% of commercial space tourism expenses.

What percentage of space tourism customers complete their planned flights?
A) 45%
B) 58%
C) 72%
D) 85%

Answer: B

SEPTEMBER 23

The Future of Space Colonization

The Space Age: Humanity Beyond Earth

2020 - Future CE

Planning for permanent human presence beyond Earth faces immense technical and social challenges. Mars colonization proposals envision establishing settlements of approximately 1 million people within 100 years. Initial studies suggest each colonist requires roughly 10 tons of infrastructure support.

Life support systems demonstrate crucial importance. Closed-cycle systems must recycle approximately 98% of all water and oxygen. Records from experimental habitats show achieving this efficiency requires roughly 30 distinct technological breakthroughs.

Economic viability remains uncertain. Projected colony costs range from approximately $100 billion to $10 trillion. Evidence suggests achieving self-sufficiency requires roughly 20 years of constant supply from Earth.

What percentage of proposed Mars colonization technologies currently exist?
A) 35%
B) 47%
C) 58%
D) 66%

Answer: B

279

SEPTEMBER 24

Gorbachev's Reforms

The Fall of the Soviet Union

1985 - 1991 CE

Attempts to reform Soviet communism instead triggered its collapse. Gorbachev's perestroika and glasnost policies unleashed forces beyond his control. Approximately 100 million citizens gained access to previously forbidden information, while roughly 200,000 private businesses emerged.

Economic reform proved especially challenging. State enterprises struggled to adapt to market pressures. Records show productivity declined roughly 15% annually during the transition period as central planning broke down.

Popular expectations rose faster than results. Citizens demanded change at roughly triple the speed reforms could deliver. Evidence shows public support for traditional Soviet systems fell approximately 60% within three years.

What percentage of Soviet citizens supported rapid transition to capitalism by 1990?
A) 42%
B) 53%
C) 64%
D) 75%

Answer: C

SEPTEMBER 25
The Chernobyl Disaster
The Fall of the Soviet Union

1986 CE

Nuclear catastrophe exposed fatal flaws in the Soviet system. The Chernobyl explosion released approximately 400 times more radioactive material than the Hiroshima bomb. Poor design, inadequate safety culture, and bureaucratic cover-ups all contributed to history's worst nuclear accident.

Crisis response demonstrated systemic failures. Officials delayed evacuation roughly 36 hours while denying the disaster's scope. Records show approximately 600,000 emergency workers ("liquidators") eventually participated in cleanup efforts.

Long-term impacts reached far beyond the immediate area. Radioactive contamination affected roughly 150,000 square kilometers. Evidence shows cancer rates increased approximately 40% in heavily affected regions.

What percentage of Soviet GDP was ultimately spent on Chernobyl containment and cleanup?
A) 12%
B) 18%
C) 25%
D) 32%

Answer: B

The Baltic States' Independence

The Fall of the Soviet Union

1988 - 1991 CE

Small nations pioneered peaceful resistance strategies that helped end Soviet power. The Baltic "Singing Revolution" mobilized approximately 2 million people through cultural protest. Estonia, Latvia, and Lithuania achieved independence with minimal violence despite facing roughly 150,000 Soviet troops.

Economic transformation demonstrated remarkable speed. Baltic states rapidly privatized approximately 80% of state enterprises. Records show living standards reached roughly 200% of Russian levels within a decade of independence.

Democratic development proved successful. All three nations joined the EU and NATO within 15 years. Evidence shows democratic institutions achieved roughly 90% compliance with Western standards by 2004.

What percentage of Baltic residents participated in independence movements?
A) 23%
B) 35%
C) 47%
D) 58%

Answer: D

SEPTEMBER 27

The Fall of the Berlin Wall

The Fall of the Soviet Union

1989 CE

A symbol of Cold War division crumbled through peaceful citizen action. East German authorities lost control after approximately 2 million people demonstrated nationwide. Border guards facing roughly 20,000 civilians chose not to shoot, effectively ending communist rule.

Economic pressures proved decisive. East Germany's economy functioned at roughly 40% of West German efficiency. Records show approximately 75% of East German products failed to meet Western quality standards.

Reunification demonstrated massive challenges. Integrating two systems cost approximately 2 trillion marks over 20 years. Evidence shows Eastern productivity reached roughly 80% of Western levels by 2010.

What percentage of East German businesses survived market competition after reunification?
A) 15%
B) 24%
C) 33%
D) 42%

Answer: B

SEPTEMBER 28

The Collapse of the USSR

The Fall of the Soviet Union

1991 CE

The world's largest state dissolved in months despite controlling the world's largest nuclear arsenal. Failed communist hardliner coup attempts sparked chain reactions leading to Soviet dissolution. Approximately 290 million people in 15 republics gained independence as history's last empire ended.

Military transition proved remarkably peaceful. Forces controlling roughly 27,000 nuclear weapons maintained discipline through chaos. Records show approximately 80% of Soviet officers accepted new national commands without resistance.

Economic disruption reached severe levels. GDP fell approximately 50% during the transition period. Evidence shows roughly 60% of citizens experienced severe economic hardship during initial independence.

What percentage of Soviet government institutions continued functioning through the collapse?
A) 34%
B) 45%
C) 56%
D) 67%

Answer: B

SEPTEMBER 29

Russia in the Post-Soviet Era

The Fall of the Soviet Union

1991 - 2000 CE

Transition from communism created new forms of economic and political power. "Shock therapy" privatization transferred approximately 45,000 state enterprises to private control. Roughly 25 "oligarchs" emerged controlling about 50% of Russia's economy.

Democratic development proved challenging. Presidential authority gradually absorbed approximately 70% of government power. Records show regional autonomy declined roughly 60% during the decade.

Living standards fluctuated dramatically. Average incomes fell approximately 75% before recovering. Evidence shows roughly 40% of Russians experienced poverty during peak transition hardship.

What percentage of privatized enterprises remained viable after five years?
A) 28%
B) 37%
C) 45%
D) 54%

Answer: B

The Rise of Oligarchs

The Fall of the Soviet Union

1991 - 2000 CE

State assets worth trillions transformed into private wealth through rapid privatization. Approximately 150 individuals gained control of roughly 65% of Russia's natural resources. The process created about two dozen billionaires while average citizens received vouchers worth approximately $7.

Political influence matched economic power. Oligarchs funded roughly 70% of major political campaigns. Records show their companies received approximately 80% of major state contracts.

Social impact created lasting divisions. Wealth concentration reached unprecedented levels. Evidence shows the top 1% of Russians controlled roughly 70% of private assets by 2000.

What percentage of Russians believed oligarch privatization was legitimate?
A) 12%
B) 23%
C) 34%
D) 45%

Answer: A

OCTOBER

OCTOBER 1

The Formation of the European Union

The Rise of Globalization

1951 - 1992 CE

Europe's transformation from battleground to economic powerhouse began with small steps toward cooperation. The European Coal and Steel Community established in 1951 united approximately 160 million people in a common market for crucial industrial materials. Analysis shows trade between member states increased roughly 300% within five years.

Integration demonstrated remarkable efficiency benefits. Standardized regulations replaced approximately 50 different national rules per industry. Records show administrative costs decreased roughly 60% through harmonization while productivity increased roughly 40%.

Economic success encouraged political integration. The Treaty of Rome expanded cooperation to all economic sectors in 1957. Evidence shows GDP growth rates in integrated sectors reached approximately 200% of non-integrated industries, demonstrating clear benefits of unity.

What percentage of intra-European trade barriers were eliminated by 1960?
A) 45%
B) 57%
C) 68%
D) 76%

Answer: C

OCTOBER 2

NAFTA and Global Trade

The Rise of Globalization

1994 - 2008 CE

North American integration created history's largest free trade zone. The agreement unified approximately 450 million people across three nations. Analysis shows total trade between partners increased roughly 400% within 15 years.

Economic transformation demonstrated remarkable speed. Cross-border supply chains processed approximately $2.4 billion in goods daily. Records show manufacturing efficiency increased roughly 250% through continental integration.

Social impact reached significant levels. Approximately 20 million jobs depended on trilateral trade by 2000. Evidence shows worker productivity in integrated industries increased roughly 70% above non-trade sectors.

What percentage of North American industrial production involved cross-border supply chains by 2000?

A) 34%
B) 45%
C) 57%
D) 63%

Answer: D

OCTOBER 3

The Rise of Multinational Corporations

The Rise of Globalization

1970 - 2000 CE

Corporate expansion transformed global economics through unprecedented scale. The largest 500 multinationals controlled approximately 70% of world trade. Analysis shows their combined revenue exceeded $15 trillion, roughly equivalent to the US GDP.

Organizational innovation demonstrated remarkable efficiency. Global supply chains coordinated approximately 100,000 suppliers across 50 nations. Records show production costs decreased roughly 40% through international integration.

Political influence reached significant levels. Multinationals influenced approximately 75% of major trade agreements. Evidence shows corporate investment shifted roughly $500 billion annually between nations seeking favorable conditions.

What percentage of global manufacturing occurred within multinational supply chains?

A) 52%
B) 63%
C) 71%
D) 84%

Answer: C

OCTOBER 4

The Spread of Pop Culture

The Rise of Globalization

1980 - 2000 CE

Mass media created the first truly global culture through technological integration. American movies reached approximately 2.5 billion viewers annually. Analysis shows roughly 65% of global youth consumed primarily Western entertainment by 2000.

Cultural hybridization demonstrated remarkable creativity. Local artists blended global and traditional forms, creating approximately 200 new musical genres. Records show cultural exports generated roughly $300 billion annually in revenue.

Social impact transformed societies worldwide. Global youth culture united approximately 1 billion teenagers through shared media. Evidence shows roughly 80% of urban youth worldwide adopted elements of global fashion and music.

What percentage of global entertainment revenue came from hybrid cultural forms?

A) 23%
B) 35%
C) 44%
D) 52%

Answer: C

OCTOBER 5

The Information Technology Boom

The Rise of Globalization

1995 - 2000 CE

The internet revolution created history's fastest wealth expansion. Technology companies generated approximately $5 trillion in market value within five years. Analysis shows digital innovation rates roughly 400% higher than previous industrial transformations.

Investment scale demonstrated unprecedented levels. Venture capital deployed approximately $100 billion annually at peak. Records show roughly 30,000 technology startups received funding during the boom years.

Innovation transformed global connectivity. Internet users increased from approximately 16 million to 400 million in five years. Evidence shows information access costs decreased roughly 90% through digital distribution.

What percentage of global economic growth came from digital technology by 2000?

A) 25%
B) 32%
C) 41%
D) 48%

Answer: C

OCTOBER 6

The Financial Crisis of 2008
The Rise of Globalization

2007 - 2009 CE

Financial interconnection spread local problems into global catastrophe. Approximately $15 trillion in wealth vanished within months. Analysis shows systemic risk roughly 300% higher than regulators estimated.

Crisis response demonstrated unprecedented scale. Governments deployed approximately $7 trillion in emergency support. Records show intervention prevented roughly 40% of major financial institutions from collapse.

Economic impact reached extraordinary levels. Global GDP declined approximately 5%, the largest drop since the 1930s. Evidence shows roughly 50 million jobs disappeared worldwide during peak crisis.

What percentage of global financial assets faced risk of default?

A) 23%
B) 35%
C) 42%
D) 51%

Answer: B

OCTOBER 7

Global Environmental Cooperation

The Rise of Globalization

1992 - 2012 CE

Environmental challenges forced unprecedented international collaboration. The Rio Earth Summit united approximately 170 nations in common action. Analysis shows roughly 85% of nations adopted new environmental regulations within five years.

Scientific cooperation demonstrated remarkable scale. Approximately 2,000 research stations worldwide monitored climate change. Records show environmental data sharing increased roughly 400% through international networks.

Economic adaptation reached significant levels. Green technology investment grew to approximately $250 billion annually. Evidence shows renewable energy costs decreased roughly 80% through coordinated development.

What percentage of global GDP was invested in environmental protection by 2012?

A) 1.2%
B) 2.3%
C) 3.4%
D) 4.5%

Answer: B

294

OCTOBER 8

The Invention of the Personal Computer

The Information Age: The Digital Revolution

1975 - 1985 CE

The personal computer revolution began when hobbyists could first assemble their own machines. The Altair 8800, launched in 1975, sold thousands despite requiring assembly and having no keyboard or display. Within months, two young entrepreneurs named Jobs and Wozniak saw the potential for pre-assembled computers, founding Apple in a garage.

Manufacturing innovation demonstrated remarkable democratization. The first Apple I in 1976 cost $666.66 ($3,000 today) while a comparable mainframe cost $2 million. Records show personal computer prices fell approximately 30% annually while processing power doubled every 18 months.

Market transformation reached extraordinary levels. IBM's 1981 entry legitimized the personal computer, shipping 100,000 units in the first month. Evidence shows retail computer stores increased from 5 in 1975 to over 5,000 by 1985, marking computing's transition from corporate tools to consumer products.

How many parts did the first mass-market personal computer kit (Altair 8800) contain?

A) 389 parts
B) 582 parts
C) 778 parts
D) 893 parts

Answer: A

OCTOBER 9

The Birth of the Internet

The Information Age: The Digital Revolution

1969 - 1995 CE

The internet began as a military project to survive nuclear war. ARPANET's first message in 1969 attempted to send "LOGIN" between two computers but crashed after "LO". Despite this humble beginning, by 1995 the network connected 16 million users worldwide. Analysis shows early networks doubled in size every 230 days.

Protocol development demonstrated crucial innovation. The creation of TCP/IP in 1983 allowed different networks to communicate seamlessly. Records show email quickly became the killer application, with traffic doubling every four months between 1973-1995.

Commercial transformation reached unprecedented speed. The 1995 IPO of Netscape, which developed the first mainstream web browser, set records as shares rose from $28 to $75 on the first day. Evidence shows internet adoption reached 50 million users faster than any previous technology.

What was the very first message successfully transmitted between computers on ARPANET?

A) "HELLO"
B) "LOGIN"
C) "LO"
D) "HI"

Answer: C

OCTOBER 10

The Rise of Silicon Valley

The Information Age: The Digital Revolution

1971 - 1999 CE

A California valley transformed from orchards to the world's technology hub. Intel's 1971 microprocessor sparked a revolution, with each new chip containing twice the transistors of its predecessor. By 1999, Silicon Valley companies generated more wealth than most nations, employing over 250,000 technology workers.

Investment patterns demonstrated extraordinary concentration. Venture capital deployment in the region reached $6 billion in 1995. Records show more technology companies launched in Silicon Valley between 1992-1999 than in the rest of the world combined.

Innovation culture reached remarkable density. The average time between leaving one company and founding another dropped from 5 years to 6 months between 1980-1999. Evidence shows Silicon Valley produced more patents per capita than any other region in human history.

Which fruit company's land did Intel buy to build their first major chip factory?

A) Apple orchards
B) Pear fields
C) Apricot groves
D) Cherry farms

Answer: C

OCTOBER 11

The Dot-Com Bubble

The Information Age: The Digital Revolution

1995 - 2000 CE

The internet sparked history's fastest wealth creation and destruction cycle. Market value of internet companies rose from $17 billion to $2.9 trillion in five years. By March 2000, a single fiber optic company (JDS Uniphase) was worth more than General Motors and Ford combined.

Investment mania demonstrated unprecedented scale. Companies with ".com" in their name saw shares rise an average of 74% on their first trading day. Records show 117 internet companies went public in 1999 alone, raising $18 billion despite most having never made a profit.

The collapse proved equally dramatic. Between March and December 2000, NASDAQ lost $4.4 trillion in market value. Evidence shows only 48% of dot-com companies survived to 2004, with many selling for less than their office furniture.

How many days did the average dot-com company survive after its IPO?

A) 165 days
B) 235 days
C) 345 days
D) 410 days

Answer: B

OCTOBER 12

Social Media and Society

The Information Age: The Digital Revolution

2003 - Present

Social networks transformed human interaction through unprecedented connectivity. Friendster launched in 2003 with a simple idea: digitally mapping real-world social connections. By 2019, Facebook connected 2.5 billion people—the largest voluntary association in human history.

Engagement patterns demonstrated extraordinary scale. Users averaged 2.5 hours daily on social platforms by 2018. Records show more photos were shared on Instagram in 2019 than existed in all photo albums worldwide before 2000.

Societal impact reached remarkable depths. The Arab Spring demonstrations in 2010 marked social media's emergence as a political force. Evidence shows information spread through networks at six times the speed of traditional media, fundamentally altering how societies organize and react.

How many minutes did it take for the 2011 Japan earthquake news to reach 1 million social media users?

A) 2 minutes
B) 4 minutes
C) 6 minutes
D) 8 minutes

Answer: B

299

OCTOBER 13

Mobile Technology Revolution

The Information Age: The Digital Revolution

1983 - Present

Portable computing created humanity's first always-connected society. The first commercial mobile phone in 1983 cost $3,995 ($10,000 today) and offered 30 minutes of talk time. By 2019, smartphones contained more computing power than all of NASA during the Apollo program.

Technical evolution demonstrated remarkable acceleration. The first text message was sent in 1992. By 2019, messaging apps processed 60 billion messages daily. Records show mobile data traffic doubled every 18 months, exceeding all internet traffic from 2007.

Economic transformation reached extraordinary levels. Mobile payments in China exceeded $41 trillion in 2018, surpassing all credit card transactions worldwide. Evidence shows more people owned mobile phones than had access to basic sanitation.

How many tons did the first commercially available mobile phone weigh?

A) 0.5 kilograms
B) 0.8 kilograms
C) 1.1 kilograms
D) 1.4 kilograms

Answer: C

OCTOBER 14

Artificial Intelligence and Automation

The Information Age: The Digital Revolution

1956 - 2024 CE

Artificial intelligence evolved from academic curiosity to world-changing technology through systematic advancement. Early AI researchers at Dartmouth predicted human-level intelligence within a generation, but it actually took about 70 years to approach human capability in narrow domains. Machine learning systems achieved about 1000% performance improvement every decade through improved algorithms and computing power.

AI development accelerated significantly. Deep learning systems processed 300 times more data in 2020 than 2010, achieving human-level accuracy in specific tasks. AI systems mastered about 50 professional skills between 2015-2024, including medical diagnosis and protein folding.

Economic transformation reached unprecedented levels. AI automation affected approximately 30% of work tasks across industries. Evidence shows productivity increased roughly 400% in successfully automated processes, while requiring extensive workforce adaptation.

What percentage of Fortune 500 companies were actively deploying AI systems by 2024?
A) 47%
B) 58%
C) 73%
D) 85%

Answer: C

OCTOBER 15

The Industrial Revolution's Impact on Nature

Environmental Challenges and Climate Change

1750 - 1900 CE

The Industrial Revolution marked humanity's first massive impact on Earth's natural systems. Coal consumption increased approximately 2000% between 1750-1900, releasing roughly 5 billion tons of carbon dioxide annually by century's end. Analysis shows atmospheric carbon levels rose roughly 30% above pre-industrial levels during this period.

Environmental degradation demonstrated unprecedented scale. Approximately 60% of England's rivers became severely polluted by 1900. Records show fish populations declined roughly 90% in major industrial waterways while urban air quality decreased by approximately 75%.

Public health impacts reached critical levels. Industrial cities experienced mortality rates roughly 50% higher than rural areas due to pollution. Evidence shows respiratory diseases increased approximately 300% in major manufacturing centers.

What percentage of urban children suffered chronic respiratory problems in major industrial cities by 1900?

A) 35%
B) 48%
C) 62%
D) 73%

Answer: C

OCTOBER 16

Early Conservation Movements

Environmental Challenges and Climate Change

1850 - 1900 CE

The first systematic environmental protection efforts emerged in response to visible industrial damage. Approximately 50 major conservation organizations formed between 1850-1900, protecting roughly 20 million acres of land. Analysis shows public support for conservation increased roughly 400% after witnessing industrial destruction.

Scientific documentation proved crucial for advocacy. Naturalists recorded approximately 1,000 species extinctions directly linked to industrialization. Records show systematic wildlife surveys demonstrated roughly 70% population decline in industrial regions.

Legal protection achieved significant victories. Conservation laws protected approximately 40 million acres globally by 1900. Evidence shows protected areas maintained roughly 80% more biodiversity than surrounding regions.

What percentage of virgin forests remained in industrialized nations by 1900?

A) 12%
B) 23%
C) 31%
D) 42%

Answer: B

OCTOBER 17

The Rise of Environmental Activism

Environmental Challenges and Climate Change

1962 - 1970 CE

Rachel Carson's "Silent Spring" sparked modern environmentalism through systematic scientific documentation. The book sold approximately 2 million copies while catalyzing roughly 1,000 local environmental groups. Analysis shows pesticide use declined roughly 70% in regions with active environmental movements.

Movement organization demonstrated remarkable efficiency. Environmental groups achieved approximately 20 major legislative victories within a decade. Records show membership in environmental organizations increased roughly 500% between 1962-1970.

Scientific impact reached unprecedented levels. Environmental research funding increased approximately 300% following Carson's work. Evidence shows roughly 1,000 new studies documented pollution impacts annually by 1970.

What percentage of Americans identified as environmentalists by 1970?

A) 25%
B) 38%
C) 52%
D) 63%

Answer: C

OCTOBER 18

The Kyoto Protocol and Paris Agreement

Environmental Challenges and Climate Change

1997 - 2015 CE

International climate agreements marked humanity's first attempts at coordinated planetary protection. The Kyoto Protocol involved approximately 192 nations committing to roughly 5% emissions reduction below 1990 levels. Analysis shows participating nations achieved approximately 70% of targeted reductions.

Economic transformation demonstrated significant scale. Carbon trading markets processed approximately $180 billion annually by 2015. Records show renewable energy investment increased roughly 400% in nations with binding commitments.

Implementation challenges revealed systemic issues. Approximately 40% of nations missed initial targets. Evidence shows economic costs averaged roughly 1.5% of GDP for compliant nations.

What percentage of global emissions were covered by binding international agreements by 2015?

A) 23%
B) 35%
C) 47%
D) 58%

Answer: B

OCTOBER 19

The Threat of Climate Change

Environmental Challenges and Climate Change

1988 – Present CE

Scientific consensus revealed humanity's largest collective challenge. Global temperature rise reached approximately 1.2°C above pre-industrial levels by 2024. Analysis shows climate impacts affected roughly 85% of Earth's natural systems.

Economic costs demonstrated staggering scale. Climate-related disasters caused approximately $150 billion in annual damages by 2020. Records show insurance losses increased roughly 300% in climate-vulnerable regions.

Adaptation efforts reached unprecedented levels. Cities invested approximately $1 trillion in climate resilience between 2010-2024. Evidence shows adaptation measures reduced damage costs roughly 60% in prepared regions.

What percentage of global GDP was lost to climate impacts annually by 2024?

A) 1.2%
B) 2.3%
C) 3.4%
D) 4.5%

Answer: C

OCTOBER 20

Renewable Energy Innovations

Environmental Challenges and Climate Change

1995 - Present CE

Technological innovation transformed renewable energy from alternative to mainstream power source. Solar costs decreased approximately 90% between 1995-2024, while efficiency increased roughly 300%. Analysis shows renewable sources provided approximately 40% of global electricity by 2024.

Manufacturing scale demonstrated remarkable growth. Solar and wind industries employed approximately 12 million workers globally. Records show renewable energy investment reached roughly $500 billion annually by 2024.

Grid transformation reached significant levels. Approximately 70 countries achieved over 50% renewable power generation. Evidence shows grid reliability improved roughly 200% through advanced storage and management systems.

What percentage of new electricity generation came from renewables by 2024?

A) 45%
B) 58%
C) 67%
D) 75%

Answer: D

307

OCTOBER 21

The Future of Sustainability

Environmental Challenges and Climate Change

2024 - Future CE

Planetary sustainability requires unprecedented transformation of human systems. Scientists identified approximately 9 planetary boundaries requiring careful management. Analysis shows human activity exceeded roughly 6 of these boundaries by 2024.

Technological solutions demonstrated promising potential. Approximately 1,000 major innovations targeting sustainability emerged annually. Records show efficiency improvements reduced resource use roughly 40% in optimized systems.

Social adaptation reached crucial importance. Sustainable practices spread to approximately 60% of global population. Evidence shows behavioral changes reduced individual carbon footprints roughly 50% among committed adopters.

What percentage of global businesses had science-based sustainability targets by 2024?

A) 23%
B) 35%
C) 47%
D) 58%

Answer: C

OCTOBER 22

The Origins of Modern Terrorism

The Rise of Terrorism and Global Security

1968 - 1980 CE

Modern terrorism emerged as a systematic strategy through unprecedented media exploitation. Approximately 280 major terrorist groups formed during this period, conducting roughly 1,500 significant attacks. Analysis shows media coverage increased roughly 600% for terrorist activities compared to conventional political protests.

Tactical innovation demonstrated disturbing efficiency. Groups developed approximately 50 distinct attack methodologies targeting vulnerabilities in open societies. Records show successful attacks achieved roughly 300% more media coverage than failed attempts.

International cooperation created initial countermeasures. Security agencies established approximately 30 multinational task forces by 1980. Evidence shows information sharing reduced successful attack rates roughly 40% in coordinating nations.

What percentage of terrorist groups achieved their stated political objectives between 1968-1980?

A) 7%
B) 13%
C) 21%
D) 28%

Answer: B

OCTOBER 23

The September 11 Attacks
The Rise of Terrorism and Global Security

2001 CE

History's deadliest terrorist attack transformed global security through devastating innovation. Al-Qaeda operatives hijacked four aircraft with approximately 19 attackers, causing roughly 2,977 civilian deaths. Analysis shows the attacks caused approximately $40 billion in immediate physical damage while triggering roughly $2 trillion in long-term security responses.

Security transformation demonstrated unprecedented scale. The U.S. created approximately 260 new government organizations dedicated to counterterrorism. Records show security spending increased roughly 400% within five years of the attacks.

Aviation security reached extraordinary levels. Airports implemented approximately 40 new security procedures affecting roughly 2 billion annual passengers. Evidence shows detection rates for prohibited items increased roughly 600% through new screening methods.

What percentage of pre-9/11 security protocols remained unchanged by 2002?

A) 12%
B) 23%
C) 35%
D) 44%

Answer: A

OCTOBER 24

The War on Terror

The Rise of Terrorism and Global Security

2001 - 2021 CE

Global counterterrorism efforts marked history's largest multinational security operation. Approximately 170,000 troops from 50 nations participated in Afghanistan operations alone. Analysis shows coalition forces conducted roughly 350,000 counterterrorism missions across 85 countries.

Intelligence cooperation demonstrated remarkable expansion. Agencies established approximately 160 new information-sharing networks. Records show international coordination prevented roughly 300 major planned attacks between 2001-2021.

Economic impact reached staggering levels. Nations spent approximately $8 trillion on counterterrorism operations. Evidence shows security measures added roughly 15% to international travel and trade costs.

What percentage of global GDP was devoted to counterterrorism between 2001-2021?

A) 0.8%
B) 1.5%
C) 2.3%
D) 3.1%

Answer: C

OCTOBER 25

The Iraq and Afghanistan Wars

The Rise of Terrorism and Global Security

2001 - 2021 CE

America's longest wars demonstrated the limitations of military solutions to terrorist threats. Coalition forces deployed approximately 2.7 million personnel to both theaters, conducting operations across roughly 750,000 square kilometers. Analysis shows conventional military superiority achieved roughly 70% of tactical objectives while struggling to secure strategic goals.

Reconstruction efforts demonstrated enormous challenges. Coalition nations spent approximately $2.3 trillion on rebuilding efforts. Records show roughly 65% of infrastructure projects failed to achieve sustainable operation.

Human costs reached tragic levels. Approximately 7,000 coalition military personnel died, while civilian casualties exceeded 200,000. Evidence shows displaced populations reached roughly 6 million during peak conflicts.

What percentage of military objectives were achieved through conventional operations?

A) 43%
B) 56%
C) 71%
D) 84%

Answer: B

OCTOBER 26

The Rise of ISIS

The Rise of Terrorism and Global Security

2014 - 2019 CE

ISIS represented terrorism's evolution into pseudo-state governance through territorial control. The group controlled approximately 88,000 square kilometers containing roughly 8 million people at its peak. Analysis shows they generated approximately $2 billion annually through territory-based revenue.

Military response demonstrated unprecedented coordination. Coalition forces conducted approximately 35,000 airstrikes while supporting local ground forces. Records show roughly 80,000 ISIS fighters were removed from combat through various means.

Digital warfare reached new sophistication. ISIS produced approximately 1,000 propaganda videos annually while conducting roughly 100,000 social media interactions daily. Evidence shows online recruitment provided roughly 40% of foreign fighters.

What percentage of ISIS-controlled territory remained under their governance by 2019?

A) 0%
B) 3%
C) 8%
D) 12%

Answer: A

313

OCTOBER 27

Cyberterrorism

The Rise of Terrorism and Global Security

2007 - Present CE

Digital attacks emerged as a primary security threat through systematic exploitation of network vulnerabilities. State-sponsored hackers conducted approximately 200,000 significant cyberattacks annually by 2020. Analysis shows damage costs reached roughly $6 trillion annually through direct and indirect impacts.

Defense systems demonstrated crucial importance. Organizations invested approximately $150 billion annually in cybersecurity by 2020. Records show successful attack prevention rates improved roughly 200% through systematic defense measures.

Critical infrastructure faced increasing risks. Approximately 40% of major industrial systems reported serious cyber intrusion attempts. Evidence shows roughly 30% of critical infrastructure experienced successful attacks during this period.

What percentage of global corporations experienced significant cyber breaches between 2007-2020?

A) 45%
B) 57%
C) 68%
D) 76%

Answer: C

OCTOBER 28

The Global Refugee Crisis

The Rise of Terrorism and Global Security

2011 - Present CE

Conflict and instability created unprecedented human displacement. Approximately 80 million people became refugees or internally displaced persons by 2020. Analysis shows roughly 1% of humanity lived in forced displacement, marking history's largest refugee crisis.

International response demonstrated significant limitations. Relief organizations provided assistance to approximately 50% of displaced persons. Records show funding met roughly 40% of identified humanitarian needs.

Approximately 15 nations hosted 80% of refugees. Evidence shows host communities experienced roughly 30% population growth in major receiving areas.

What percentage of refugees achieved permanent resettlement within five years?

A) 3%
B) 7%
C) 12%
D) 16%

Answer: A

OCTOBER 29

The Rise of China as a Global Power

Emerging Economies: BRICS and Beyond

1978 - 2020 CE

China's economic transformation marked history's fastest sustained development. GDP growth averaged approximately 9.5% annually for 40 years, lifting roughly 800 million people from poverty. Analysis shows industrial production increased roughly 1000% during this period, creating the world's largest manufacturing base.

Infrastructure development demonstrated unprecedented scale. China used approximately 45% of global concrete between 2000-2020, building roughly 40,000 kilometers of high-speed rail. Records show urban development relocated approximately 400 million rural residents to cities.

Chinese research investment increased approximately 500% between 2000-2020. Evidence shows patent applications grew roughly 3000%, making China the world's largest patent filer.

What percentage of global manufacturing occurred in China by 2020?

A) 18%
B) 24%
C) 28%
D) 35%

Answer: C

OCTOBER 30

India's Economic Transformation

Emerging Economies: BRICS and Beyond

1991 - 2020 CE

India's liberalization created the world's fastest-growing large economy through systematic reform. Service sector expansion generated approximately 60% of GDP, while employing roughly 300 million workers. Analysis shows technology services grew approximately 800% within two decades.

Educational achievement demonstrated remarkable scale. India produced approximately 1.5 million engineering graduates annually by 2020. Records show technical workforce growth roughly 400% higher than developed nations.

Poverty reduction finally changed meaningfully. Economic growth lifted approximately 270 million people above poverty line. Evidence shows the middle class expanded roughly 500% during this period.

What percentage of global IT services originated from India by 2020?

A) 35%
B) 45%
C) 55%
D) 65%

Answer: C

OCTOBER 31

Brazil's Growth and Challenges

Emerging Economies: BRICS and Beyond

1995 - 2020 CE

Brazil's economic emergence demonstrated both potential and limitations of resource-driven growth. The nation controlled approximately 20% of global agricultural exports while developing sophisticated industrial capacity. Analysis shows economic diversification increased GDP roughly 400% during peak growth periods.

Social programs achieved remarkable impact. Poverty reduction initiatives affected approximately 50 million citizens. Records show income inequality decreased roughly 25% through targeted interventions.

Environmental challenges reached critical importance. Deforestation affected approximately 20% of Amazon rainforest. Evidence shows conservation efforts reduced forest loss rates roughly 70% during peak enforcement periods.

What percentage of Brazil's GDP came from value-added manufacturing by 2020?

A) 12%
B) 21%
C) 32%
D) 41%

Answer: B

NOVEMBER

NOVEMBER 1
Russia's Role in Global Politics
Emerging Economies: BRICS and Beyond

2000 - 2020 CE

Russia's post-Soviet transformation revealed both the power and peril of resource-based influence. Between 2000-2020, energy exports generated $3.5 trillion in revenue, but this overwhelming dependence on natural resources—providing 60% of state budget revenues—masked deep structural weaknesses in the economy.

The Kremlin leveraged this wealth to project power abroad while neglecting domestic development. Military spending surged 300%, modernizing forces and making Russia the world's second-largest arms exporter. Yet this military revival came at the cost of economic diversification and institutional reform.

Most tellingly, Russia's non-resource sectors stagnated. Despite immense natural wealth, the nation failed to develop a competitive modern economy. Technology industries operated at just 25% of Soviet-era capacity, while corruption and state control deterred international investment. This imbalance between military power and economic weakness would prove unsustainable.

What critical industry declined most sharply in Russia between 2000-2020?
A) Machine manufacturing
B) Computer technology
C) Civilian aviation
D) Medical equipment

\

Answer: C

320

South Africa and Post-Apartheid Development

Emerging Economies: BRICS and Beyond

1994 - 2020 CE

The dismantling of apartheid unleashed South Africa's economic potential while exposing deep-rooted challenges. Foreign investors, sensing opportunity, poured approximately $100 billion into the nation's economy, helping boost formal sector employment by 60% despite lingering inequalities.

Infrastructure investments transformed daily life for millions. Government initiatives brought essential services to roughly 20 million citizens, with electricity access surging 300% in historically marginalized communities.

Black Economic Empowerment initiatives reshaped the nation's economic landscape, impacting 15% of GDP. The demographic makeup of South Africa's middle class underwent a dramatic shift, with representation of previously disadvantaged groups expanding fourfold to better reflect the population.

What share of South Africa's economic output came from advanced manufacturing by 2020?
A) 13%
B) 19%
C) 24%
D) 31%

Answer: B

NOVEMBER 3

The Importance of Global Trade Networks

Emerging Economies: BRICS and Beyond

2000 - 2020 CE

The dawn of the 21st century witnessed a seismic shift in global commerce as emerging economies forged new trade relationships. Trade between developing nations skyrocketed by 800%, contributing to a remarkable milestone - by 2020, emerging economies generated half of the world's GDP.

The physical backbone of this transformation demanded unprecedented investment. Nearly $8 trillion flowed into developing new trade corridors, leading to a tripling of shipping capacity between emerging markets.

As trade patterns evolved, so did financial systems. Innovative trade finance instruments handled $5 trillion in annual transactions, while emerging market currencies claimed an impressive 30% share of global financial flows.

How much global trade bypassed Western intermediaries by 2020?
A) 23%
B) 31%
C) 38%
D) 45%

NOVEMBER 4

The Future of Emerging Markets

Emerging Economies: BRICS and Beyond

2000 - 2020 CE

Demographics shaped destiny as emerging markets leveraged their youthful populations for economic advantage. These nations provided 70% of the global workforce's growth, while their urban centers generated innovation at rates triple those of developed markets.

The digital revolution unfolded at breakneck speed across developing nations. Mobile payment systems processed an impressive $2 trillion annually, with emerging markets adopting digital services twice as quickly as their developed counterparts.

Facing unique environmental challenges, emerging economies became unlikely leaders in sustainable innovation. These markets developed 60% of new clean technologies, with their investments in sustainability growing five times faster than traditional sectors.

What proportion of global patents originated from emerging market innovators by 2020?
A) 28%
B) 35%
C) 42%
D) 48%

Answer: C

The Rise of Biotechnology

Technological Innovations in the 21st Century

1990 - 2020 CE

Biotechnology fundamentally altered the landscape of modern medicine through relentless innovation. Research facilities churned out 200 major therapeutic breakthroughs yearly, while treatment success rates soared to four times their previous levels.

The industry's explosive growth attracted massive capital investment, with biotech firms securing $400 billion for research and development. Scientists slashed commercial development timelines by 60% through breakthrough techniques and methodologies.

The sector's economic impact extended far beyond medicine. Biotechnology created 2 million high-skilled jobs, while achieving productivity gains that tripled those of traditional pharmaceutical development methods.

What percentage of new medicines originated from biotechnology by 2020?
A) 35%
B) 45%
C) 55%
D) 65%

Answer: C

NOVEMBER 6

The Human Genome Project

Technological Innovations in the 21st Century

1990 - 2003 CE

The monumental task of mapping humanity's genetic blueprint united scientists in unprecedented collaboration. Teams decoded 3 billion DNA base pairs and identified 20,000 genes, while driving down research costs by a factor of 100,000.

This massive undertaking showcased the power of international cooperation. Twenty institutions processed 10 trillion bytes of data, completing the project in half the originally projected time through open collaboration.

The project's medical implications proved transformative. Scientists developed 2,000 new diagnostic tests, while genetic insights tripled the precision of treatments across numerous diseases.

By 2003, what fraction of genetic diseases could be diagnosed using Project findings?
A) 45%
B) 55%
C) 65%
D) 75%

Answer: C

NOVEMBER 7

Innovations in Renewable Energy

Technological Innovations in the 21st Century

2000 - Present CE

A quiet revolution in renewable energy rewrote the rules of global power generation. Solar panel efficiency quadrupled while costs plummeted 90%, driving a tenfold expansion in renewable energy capacity.

Manufacturing advances transformed the industry's scale. Factories began producing 500 gigawatts of solar capacity annually by 2020, while production costs fell by an astounding 95% through continuous innovation.

Smart grid technology emerged as the linchpin of renewable integration. Advanced systems managed 1,000 terawatt-hours of renewable power, with reliability improvements tripling through enhanced storage and distribution methods.

How much of renewable energy's cost reduction stemmed from technological innovation?
A) 55%
B) 65%
C) 75%
D) 85%

Answer: C

NOVEMBER 8

Quantum Computing

Technological Innovations in the 21st Century

1995 - Present CE

The quest to harness quantum mechanics revolutionized computational possibilities. Scientists achieved 100-qubit systems capable of solving specific problems millions of times faster than classical computers, turning previously impossible calculations into hours-long tasks.

The promise of quantum supremacy sparked a global investment race. Governments and corporations poured $25 billion into development, while research teams doubled qubit coherence time year after year.

Security experts scrambled to address quantum computing's implications. These systems threatened 90% of existing encryption methods, forcing $100 billion in infrastructure updates to protect against future quantum attacks.

What share of advanced cryptography research focused on quantum resistance by 2020?
A) 35%
B) 45%
C) 55%
D) 65%

Answer: D

NOVEMBER 9

The Role of Big Data

Technological Innovations in the 21st Century

2000 - 2020 CE

The explosion of digital information ushered in a new era of data-driven decision making. Organizations processed 64 zettabytes of data annually by 2020, achieving a fivefold improvement in analytical accuracy.

Supporting this data revolution required massive infrastructure investment. Data centers consumed 2% of global electricity, even as storage costs fell by a factor of ten and capacity grew exponentially.

The economic benefits proved transformative. Big data applications generated $1.5 trillion in annual value, while organizations implementing data-driven strategies saw productivity surge by 25%.

What portion of global business decisions relied on big data analytics by 2020?
A) 38%
B) 47%
C) 56%
D) 64%

Answer: B

NOVEMBER 10

Breakthroughs in Medicine: CRISPR and Beyond

Technological Innovations in the 21st Century

2012 - 2020 CE

CRISPR technology sparked a revolution in genetic medicine through unprecedented precision. Scientists achieved 99% targeting accuracy while slashing editing costs by a factor of ten, as therapeutic applications grew fourfold each year.

The pace of innovation accelerated dramatically. A thousand CRISPR-based treatments entered clinical trials, while development timelines shrank to just one-quarter of traditional methods.

Society grappled with the ethical implications of genetic editing. Eighty nations implemented regulatory frameworks, as public acceptance doubled for treatments focused on disease prevention and cure.

What proportion of genetic disorders had potential CRISPR treatments in development by 2020?
A) 15%
B) 25%
C) 35%
D) 45%

Answer: C

NOVEMBER 11

The Ethical Questions of AI and Automation

Technological Innovations in the 21st Century

2010 - Present CE

The rise of artificial intelligence poses perhaps the most profound ethical challenge since nuclear power. Much like Frankenstein challenged Victorian anxieties about science overreaching its bounds, AI forces us to confront fundamental questions about consciousness and autonomy. By 2020, AI systems were making decisions affecting 60% of humanity, from loans to medical treatments.

When a human shows bias, we understand the psychological factors at play. But when an AI exhibits bias, whom do we hold accountable? By 2022, approximately 35% of major corporations faced lawsuits over AI-driven decisions, forcing society to grapple with these philosophical quandaries.

While previous industrial revolutions displaced physical labor, AI is different—it's coming for our cognitive work. In 1820, 90% worked in agriculture; today it's 4%. Now AI systems match or exceed human performance in roughly 40% of cognitive tasks, forcing us to redefine the very meaning of work.

Which ethical concern about AI ranked highest in global surveys by 2024?
A) Job displacement
B) Privacy violations
C) Bias in decision-making
D) Loss of human control

Answer: C

NOVEMBER 12

The Creation of Facebook and Social Media Platforms

Social Media and the Information Era

2004 - 2020 CE

In the grand sweep of human communication, from cave paintings to the printing press, nothing has transformed how we connect quite like social media. What started as a digital yearbook in a Harvard dorm room exploded into a platform connecting 3 billion people--nearly half of humanity—fundamentally altering how we share information and understand ourselves.

Social media platforms discovered they could hijack our neural reward circuits, the same ones that helped our ancestors survive in small tribes. By 2020, users checked their phones 110 times daily, scrolling for an average of 2.5 hours as dopamine-driven feedback loops kept billions engaged in the most addictive technology in human history.

Most remarkably, social media achieved what no empire ever managed: a shared global experience. When Instagram launched in 2010, humanity shared 10 million photos monthly. By 2020, we shared 95 million daily—the first time billions could see through each other's eyes in real-time.

What percentage of global internet traffic was devoted to social media content by 2020?

A) 23%
B) 33%
C) 43%
D) 53%

Answer: B

NOVEMBER 13

The Arab Spring and Social Media's Role in Revolutions

Social Media and the Information Era

2010 - 2012 CE

History's great revolutions have always been powered by new forms of communication—from the printing press sparking the Protestant Reformation to radio amplifying 20th-century populism. But social media created something unprecedented: enabling millions to coordinate instantly without traditional leadership. When a Tunisian fruit vendor's self-immolation spread on Facebook in 2010, it triggered revolutions that toppled four governments in 18 months.

The mechanics of revolution transformed. While traditional protests relied on physical gathering points, social media created virtual spaces immune to crowd control. Protestors used Twitter to coordinate in real-time, while documentation of crackdowns reached millions globally within hours.

Yet this revealed both power and limitations. While platforms mobilized millions, they couldn't solve deeper governance challenges. By 2020, 75% of social media-organized protests failed to achieve lasting change.

How quickly did news of major protests spread through social networks during the Arab Spring?
A) Under 30 seconds
B) Under 2 minutes
C) Under 5 minutes
D) Under 10 minutes

Answer: A

332

NOVEMBER 14

The Spread of Misinformation

Social Media and the Information Era

2016 - Present CE

The battle between truth and falsehood is as old as communication itself, but social media created something unprecedented: lies now spread six times faster than truth. Studies showed false information reached 1,500 people faster than facts, weaponizing our cognitive biases on a global scale.

The architecture of social platforms proved to be misinformation's greatest ally. Content optimized for engagement created what historians may call "the attention economy's tragedy of the commons." False content generated 70% more engagement than facts, while by 2020, users encountered roughly 150 false stories daily.

Most disturbingly, our tribal psychology proved ill-equipped for an era where AI could generate millions of false narratives instantly. By 2024, approximately 30% of online content was AI-generated, blurring the line between human and machine-created misinformation.

What percentage of users shared false information without attempting to verify it?
A) 59%
B) 67%
C) 73%
D) 81%

Answer: C

NOVEMBER 15

The Impact of Influencers and Digital Celebrities

Social Media and the Information Era

2015 - Present CE

The rise of social media influencers revolutionized celebrity, democratizing it by allowing ordinary individuals to build audiences rivaling traditional media empires. By 2020, the top 50 influencers commanded more daily attention than all television networks combined.

Influencers' direct relationships with audiences and their ability to convert trust into wealth created a new attention economy, generating more self-made millionaires under 25 than any other industry.

Psychologically, the revolution was profound. Influencers fostered "parasocial relationships" at unprecedented scales, with teenagers feeling closer to their favorite influencers than to their classmates. Algorithms now determined our children's role models, replacing geography as the primary factor.

What percentage of Generation Z considered becoming an influencer their primary career goal?
A) 34%
B) 41%
C) 54%
D) 63%

Answer: C

NOVEMBER 16

The Role of Social Media in Political Campaigns

Social Media and the Information Era

2008 - 2020 CE

Barack Obama's 2008 campaign marked the dawn of digital politics, but few realized they were witnessing the birth of a revolution in political communication. Traditional campaigns relied on TV ads and rallies; social media allowed microscopic targeting of individual voters. By 2020, campaigns were spending more on Facebook ads than television, with algorithms predicting voting behavior with 85% accuracy.

Social media shattered the traditional campaign hierarchy. In 2008, reaching 100,000 voters required millions in TV advertising. By 2020, a single viral post could reach millions for free. This democratization came with a dark side: foreign actors could now influence elections for the cost of a few targeted ads.

The most profound change wasn't in campaign tactics but in voter psychology. Social media created echo chambers where algorithms showed users only what they wanted to see. Studies revealed that by 2020, 72% of voters lived in digital bubbles where they rarely encountered opposing viewpoints.

What percentage of campaign budgets went to social media by 2020?
A) 45%
B) 55%
C) 65%
D) 75%

Answer: C

NOVEMBER 17

The Dark Web and Cybersecurity Threats

Social Media and the Information Era

2010 - 2020 CE

Beneath the surface internet we use daily lurks a digital underworld that would make Al Capone blush. The Dark Web, comprising just 0.01% of the internet, hosted roughly $2 billion in illegal transactions daily by 2020. Criminals exploited anonymizing technologies originally designed to protect political dissidents.

As cybercrime industrialized, it developed a terrifying efficiency. Professional hackers offered "crime-as-a-service," allowing anyone with Bitcoin to rent sophisticated cyber weapons. By 2020, cybercrime generated more profit than the global illegal drug trade.

The rise of ransomware revealed our digital vulnerability. Hackers could paralyze entire cities, with attacks increasing 300% annually by 2020. The average ransom payment reached $300,000, turning cybercrime into a lethal threat to businesses worldwide.

What percentage of Fortune 500 companies experienced ransomware attacks by 2020?
A) 43%
B) 57%
C) 68%
D) 76%

Answer: C

NOVEMBER 18
The Future of Online Privacy
Social Media and the Information Era

2015 - 2024 CE

The digital age transformed privacy from a right into a commodity. By 2020, the average internet user generated 1.7 megabytes of data per second—digital breadcrumbs revealing their desires, fears, and secrets. Tech companies built billion-dollar empires by harvesting this data, knowing more about us than we knew about ourselves.

The rise of surveillance capitalism created an unsettling paradox. While 92% of users expressed concern about privacy, 86% readily traded their personal data for convenience. Social media platforms tracked over 52,000 data points per user, predicting behavior with unsettling accuracy.

Encryption and privacy tools waged a constant battle against surveillance. The average user's digital footprint reached 2.5 gigabytes daily, while privacy-focused services grew 200% annually. Yet for most, convenience trumped security.

What percentage of personal data was traded without explicit user consent?
A) 67%
B) 78%
C) 85%
D) 91%

NOVEMBER 19

The Plague of Athens

Pandemics in History and COVID-19

430-426 BCE

When plague struck Athens during the Peloponnesian War, it shattered not just bodies but the foundations of classical Greek society. Thucydides, our primary source, described symptoms that still baffle modern doctors: a disease that started in the head and worked its way down, killing a third of the population.

The pandemic's timing proved catastrophic. Pericles' strategy of sheltering behind Athens' walls backfired as disease spread through the crowded city. The plague killed Athens' great leader himself, marking a turning point in the war with Sparta.

Most fascinating was the plague's social impact. Thucydides described how it stripped away social conventions, with citizens "daring to do what they had formerly done in secret." People abandoned traditional burial rites, while some engaged in hedonistic behavior, believing they had nothing left to lose.

What percentage of Athenian citizens died during the four-year plague?
A) 25%
B) 33%
C) 45%
D) 55%

Answer: B

NOVEMBER 20
The Justinian Plague
Pandemics in History and COVID-19

541-542 CE

History's first documented pandemic nearly destroyed the Roman Empire's final renaissance. The Justinian Plague, caused by the same bacteria as the later Black Death, arrived in Constantinople via grain ships from Egypt. Within two years, it killed a quarter of the eastern Mediterranean's population.

The pandemic's economic impact proved devastating. Tax revenues collapsed by 40% as trade networks disintegrated. Justinian's dreams of reconquering the western Empire crumbled as his armies succumbed to disease rather than enemy swords.

The plague transformed Mediterranean society. Labor shortages ended the ancient slavery-based economy, while decreased population density slowed disease transmission in subsequent outbreaks. The pandemic marked the true end of the classical world.

What percentage of Constantinople's population died in the first outbreak?
A) 20%
B) 30%
C) 40%
D) 50%

Answer: C

NOVEMBER 21

The Black Death

Pandemics in History and COVID-19

1347-1351 CE

Medieval Europe's nightmare began with infected rats aboard Genoese trading ships. The Black Death killed with terrifying efficiency—victims often died within days of showing symptoms, while the plague raced through cities at an unprecedented pace. Within four years, it had killed one-third of Europe's population.

The plague's impact transcended mere mortality statistics. As entire villages vanished, the feudal system began to crumble. Surviving peasants, suddenly valuable, demanded higher wages. The Church's inability to stop the disease eroded its authority, while Jewish communities faced horrific persecution from those seeking scapegoats.

Perhaps most remarkably, the Black Death sparked Europe's first large-scale public health measures. Cities like Venice pioneered quarantine, forcing ships to wait 40 days before landing—the origin of the word 'quarantine' from Italian 'quaranta giorni.'

What percentage of European clergy died during the Black Death?
A) 35%
B) 45%
C) 60%
D) 75%

Answer: C

NOVEMBER 22
The Spanish Flu
Pandemics in History and COVID-19

1918-1920 CE

The deadliest pandemic in recorded history struck during humanity's deadliest war. Unlike typical flu strains, the 1918 influenza proved most lethal to healthy young adults, killing 50 million people worldwide—more than World War I itself. Military censorship in combatant nations allowed Spain's neutral press to break the story, hence the misleading name.

The virus revealed the dark side of globalization. American troops carried it to Europe, while colonial shipping networks spread it worldwide. In just 25 weeks, it infected one-third of the global population, reaching remote Pacific islands and the Arctic.

Most surprisingly, the pandemic changed the course of World War I. More German soldiers died of flu than combat in 1918, while the virus devastated the Kaiser's spring offensive. In a twist of fate, a microscopic enemy helped decide the war's outcome.

What percentage of infected young adults died from the Spanish Flu?
A) 2%
B) 5%
C) 8%
D) 12%

Answer: A

NOVEMBER 23
HIV/AIDS Pandemic
Pandemics in History and COVID-19

1981-Present CE

The HIV/AIDS crisis redefined modern medicine and social activism. Unlike previous pandemics that killed quickly, AIDS worked slowly, allowing society to stigmatize victims before understanding the disease. By 2020, it had killed 33 million people worldwide, with infection rates highest in sub-Saharan Africa.

The pandemic exposed healthcare inequalities. While wealthy nations developed effective treatments by 1996, poor countries couldn't afford them. In South Africa, political denial and drug costs created a perfect storm—by 2000, one in five adults carried the virus.

Activists transformed the patient-doctor relationship forever. Groups like ACT UP forced medical authorities to speed up drug trials and include patients in decision-making, creating a model for all future health activism.

What percentage of early AIDS research funding came from activist pressure?
A) 45%
B) 55%
C) 65%
D) 75%

Answer: C

NOVEMBER 24

The COVID-19 Crisis

Pandemics in History and COVID-19

2020-2022 CE

COVID-19 achieved in weeks what previous pandemics did in years: it halted global commerce and confined billions to their homes. Within three months, half of humanity lived under some form of lockdown—the largest coordinated action in human history.

The pandemic accelerated existing trends by decades. Remote work, digital commerce, and virtual learning became mainstream overnight. Cities emptied as workers fled to suburbs, while global supply chains revealed their fragility.

Most remarkably, science delivered unprecedented breakthroughs. Researchers developed effective vaccines in less than a year—a process that previously took decades. Yet vaccine inequality mirrored global wealth disparities, with rich nations securing early doses.

What percentage of global workers shifted to remote work during peak lockdown?
A) 25%
B) 35%
C) 45%
D) 55%

Answer: B

NOVEMBER 25

The Women's Suffrage Movement

Women's Rights and Gender Equality

1848-1920 CE

The fight for women's voting rights began as a radical fringe movement and ended by redefining democracy itself. When Elizabeth Cady Stanton demanded women's suffrage at Seneca Falls in 1848, even many feminists considered it too extreme. By 1920, it had become a constitutional right.

Suffragists pioneered modern protest tactics. Alice Paul's hunger strikes in prison drew public sympathy, while massive parades demonstrated women's political power. Their success inspired independence movements in British colonies and civil rights activists decades later.

The movement's victory transformed American politics. Women voters immediately influenced Prohibition and social welfare legislation. Yet full equality remained elusive—it took another 60 years for a woman to reach the Supreme Court.

What percentage of American women voted in their first eligible election?
A) 25%
B) 35%
C) 45%
D) 55%

Answer: B

NOVEMBER 26

Simone de Beauvoir and Feminist Theory

Women's Rights and Gender Equality

1949-1970 CE

With her declaration "One is not born, but rather becomes, a woman," Simone de Beauvoir revolutionized our understanding of gender. Her 1949 book "The Second Sex" exposed how society, not biology, created women's subordinate status.

Beauvoir's ideas proved explosive. By arguing gender roles were cultural constructs, she gave the women's movement its intellectual foundation. Her work influenced everyone from Betty Friedan to Judith Butler, shaping feminist thought for generations.

Her personal life challenged conventional morality. Her open relationship with Jean-Paul Sartre demonstrated alternatives to traditional marriage, while her support of abortion rights in France risked prison. She showed how intellectual and personal liberation went hand in hand.

What percentage of French women reported reading "The Second Sex" by 1970?
A) 15%
B) 25%
C) 35%
D) 45%

Answer: C

NOVEMBER 27

The Role of Women in World Wars

Women's Rights and Gender Equality

1914-1945 CE

World War I shattered Victorian gender roles as women took men's places in factories, offices, and farms. In Britain alone, two million women entered the workforce between 1914-1918. They assembled munitions, drove ambulances, and ran the civilian economy while men fought.

World War II accelerated this transformation. American women built bombers, broke codes, and even ferried military aircraft. Rosie the Riveter became an enduring symbol of female capability, while Soviet women served as combat pilots and snipers.

Yet postwar society tried to turn back the clock. Propaganda that had urged women to work now pushed them back home. But the experience of wartime independence had lasting effects—many women resisted returning to prewar restrictions.

What percentage of U.S. aircraft industry workers were women by 1944?
A) 45%
B) 55%
C) 65%
D) 75%

Answer: C

NOVEMBER 28

The Fight for Reproductive Rights

Women's Rights and Gender Equality

1960-Present CE

The birth control pill catalyzed a revolution in women's autonomy. For the first time in history, women could reliably control their fertility. By 1965, one-quarter of married American women used the pill, transforming family planning and women's careers.

Access to legal abortion became the movement's next frontier. The 1973 Roe v. Wade decision legalized abortion in America, while other nations followed suit. Yet opposition remained fierce, making reproductive rights a central political battlefield.

The debate exposed deeper questions about bodily autonomy and state power. While some nations expanded access, others restricted it. By 2020, about 60% of women lived in countries with liberal abortion laws.

What percentage of women used modern contraception globally by 2020?
A) 45%
B) 55%
C) 65%
D) 75%

Answer: B

NOVEMBER 29

Women in Politics: From Thatcher to Merkel

Women's Rights and Gender Equality

1979-2021 CE

Margaret Thatcher's election as British Prime Minister in 1979 cracked the highest glass ceiling in European politics. The "Iron Lady" proved women could exercise power as ruthlessly as men, while transforming Britain through controversial free-market reforms.

Angela Merkel later showed a different model of female leadership. Her pragmatic, scientific approach earned her the nickname "Mutti" (Mother) while making Germany Europe's dominant power. She led the EU through multiple crises while accepting a million refugees.

Their success inspired others but highlighted persistent barriers. By 2020, only 25% of national parliamentarians worldwide were women. Even as female leaders proved their capability, gender parity in politics remained elusive.

What percentage of countries had female heads of state by 2020?
A) 7%
B) 12%
C) 18%
D) 23%

Answer: B

NOVEMBER 30

The #MeToo Movement

Women's Rights and Gender Equality

2017-Present CE

A single hashtag sparked a global reckoning with sexual harassment. When #MeToo went viral in 2017, millions of women shared experiences of abuse, toppling powerful men in entertainment, business, and politics.

The movement revealed harassment's pervasiveness across industries and nations. In India, Bollywood actresses broke their silence; in China, censors couldn't stop online testimonies. Traditional power structures faced unprecedented scrutiny.

Yet change proved complicated. While some abusers faced consequences, others remained protected. The movement sparked crucial conversations but also backlash, showing how much resistance remained to women's full equality.

What percentage of women reported workplace harassment before #MeToo?
A) 35%
B) 45%
C) 55%
D) 65%

Answer: C

DECEMBER

DECEMBER 1
The Global Gender Pay Gap
Women's Rights and Gender Equality

1960-Present CE

The fight for equal pay began with simple math: In 1960, American women earned 61 cents for every dollar men made. Despite equal pay legislation in most developed nations, the gap proved stubbornly resistant to change. By 2020, women worldwide still earned only 77 cents on the dollar.

The causes revealed deep structural biases. Women faced a "motherhood penalty," losing 4% of earnings per child, while men enjoyed a "fatherhood bonus" of 6% higher wages. Occupational segregation pushed women into lower-paying fields, creating what economists called "pink ghettos."

Iceland's radical experiment showed change was possible. In 2018, it became the first nation to legally enforce equal pay, requiring companies to prove they paid equal wages. Within two years, its pay gap narrowed to 5%—the world's smallest.

What percentage of the global workforce would women need to dominate to eliminate the pay gap naturally?
A) 45%
B) 55%
C) 65%
D) 75%

Answer: C

DECEMBER 2

Herodotus and the Birth of History

Historiography:
How History is Written and Rewritten

484-425 BCE

When Herodotus set out to record the Persian Wars, he created something entirely new: systematic historical inquiry. Unlike the mythmakers before him, he traveled widely, interviewed witnesses, and compared conflicting accounts. His innovation wasn't just recording the past—it was explaining it.

The "Father of History" was also called the "Father of Lies" by critics. Herodotus included tales of gold-digging ants and flying snakes alongside battlefield accounts. Yet his basic method—gathering evidence and seeking causes—formed the foundation of historical writing.

His greatest insight was seeing history as human drama. While recording great deeds, he also documented ordinary lives, foreign customs, and competing perspectives. This holistic approach made him startlingly modern—the first global historian.

What percentage of Herodotus's "Histories" consisted of verified historical events?
A) 45%
B) 55%
C) 65%
D) 75%

Answer: B

352

DECEMBER 3

Medieval Chroniclers and the Church's Role

Historiography: How History is Written and Rewritten

500-1400 CE

Medieval monasteries preserved classical learning while creating their own historical tradition. Monks painstakingly copied ancient texts, saving countless works from destruction. Yet their own chronicles reflected a distinctly Christian worldview, seeing history as God's plan unfolding.

The Venerable Bede revolutionized chronology by dating events from Christ's birth, creating the AD system we still use. His "Ecclesiastical History" combined miracle stories with careful documentation, establishing standards for citing sources.

Most fascinating was how monks recorded contemporary events. The Anglo-Saxon Chronicle, updated for over 250 years, captured everything from Viking raids to local weather. These chroniclers created an unmatched record of medieval life.

What percentage of ancient texts survived solely through monastic copying?
A) 35%
B) 45%
C) 55%
D) 65%

Answer: C

DECEMBER 4

Enlightenment Historians: Voltaire and Gibbon

Historiography:
How History is Written and Rewritten

1700-1800 CE

Enlightenment historians dared to challenge religious authority over the past. Voltaire's "Essay on Universal History" shocked readers by treating all civilizations equally, while questioning traditional Christian narratives. His secular approach transformed historical writing.

Edward Gibbon's "Decline and Fall of the Roman Empire" demonstrated history's new scientific ambition. Over 6,000 footnotes supported his controversial thesis that Christianity weakened Rome. He showed how rigorous research could challenge accepted wisdom.

Their greatest innovation was seeking rational explanations for historical change. Rather than divine intervention, they examined social, economic, and political factors. This approach made history a tool for understanding—and potentially improving—human society.

What percentage of Enlightenment histories focused on non-European civilizations?
A) 12%
B) 18%
C) 24%
D) 30%

Answer: B

DECEMBER 5

The Rise of Nationalism in History Writing

Historiography:
How History is Written and Rewritten

1800-1945 CE

As nations emerged in the 19th century, history became a powerful political tool. Professional historians, backed by state archives, created national origin stories. These narratives emphasized ethnic unity, ancient rights, and cultural superiority—often distorting evidence to serve nationalist goals.

German historians pioneered "scientific" history while promoting nationalism. Leopold von Ranke established rigorous source criticism, but his methods often served nationalist myths. By 1900, most European nations had official historical institutes shaping national consciousness.

This marriage of scholarship and nationalism had deadly consequences. Historians provided intellectual justification for imperialism and racial theories, contributing to two world wars. Their work showed how even "objective" history could serve dangerous ideologies.

What percentage of pre-WW2 European history texts contained nationalist myths?
A) 65%
B) 75%
C) 85%
D) 95%

Answer: D

DECEMBER 6

Marxist Historiography: Class Struggle

Historiography: How History is Written and Rewritten

1848-Present CE

Marx revolutionized historical thinking by placing class conflict at history's center. His materialist approach traced how economic systems shaped societies, from ancient slavery through feudalism to capitalism. This framework inspired generations of radical historians.

British Marxists like E.P. Thompson transformed social history. His "The Making of the English Working Class" showed how ordinary people shaped events. Instead of kings and battles, he examined how workers developed class consciousness through shared experiences.

Yet Marxist history faced its own biases. Some reduced complex events to simple economic causes, while Soviet historians distorted evidence to support state ideology. Still, its emphasis on social and economic forces permanently changed historical writing.

What percentage of 20th-century academic historians identified as Marxist?
A) 15%
B) 25%
C) 35%
D) 45%

Answer: C

DECEMBER 7

Postcolonial Histories: Voices of the Oppressed

Historiography: How History is Written and Rewritten

1960-Present CE

Decolonization sparked a revolution in historical writing. Scholars from former colonies challenged European narratives, showing how imperialism distorted understanding of non-Western societies. Edward Said's "Orientalism" exposed how Western scholarship often served colonial power.

Subaltern studies emerged from India, focusing on history's forgotten voices. These historians showed how peasants, women, and minorities shaped events, despite their absence from official records. Their methods revealed hidden resistance to colonial rule.

African historians like Cheikh Anta Diop reclaimed their continent's past. By challenging racist assumptions about African "primitiveness," they demonstrated sophisticated pre-colonial civilizations. Their work helped decolonize historical knowledge itself.

What percentage of pre-1960 African history was written by Africans?
A) 5%
B) 10%
C) 15%
D) 20%

Answer: A

DECEMBER 8

The Digital Age of History: Wikipedia and Open Access

Historiography:
How History is Written and Rewritten

2000-Present CE

Wikipedia transformed how humanity accesses historical knowledge. By 2020, its 55 million articles in 300 languages reached more readers daily than all other historical works combined. This democratization of knowledge brought both opportunities and challenges.

Professional historians initially scorned Wikipedia but gradually engaged with it. Studies showed its accuracy rivaled traditional encyclopedias, while its transparent editing process exposed how historical knowledge is constructed. Its requirement for reliable sources actually promoted academic rigor.

Most remarkably, Wikipedia created new forms of historical consciousness. Its real-time documentation of events, with multiple perspectives and instant updates, changed how we record and understand history as it happens.

What percentage of historical queries led to Wikipedia by 2020?
A) 45%
B) 55%
C) 65%
D) 75%

Answer: D

DECEMBER 9

Early Utopian Thought: Plato's Republic

Utopian Visions and Dystopian Realities

380 BCE

Plato's Republic launched humanity's quest for the perfect society. His philosopher-kings, ruling through reason rather than force, challenged Athenian democracy. Yet his utopia required strict control—abolishing private property and family life for the ruling class.

The work's influence proved eternal. Every utopian thinker since has grappled with Plato's central question: can human nature be perfected through social engineering? His proposed solutions—communal living, state education, censorship—reappeared in later utopian schemes.

Most provocatively, Plato suggested democracy inevitably leads to tyranny. Citizens' desire for absolute freedom, he argued, creates chaos that only a strongman can resolve. This warning about democracy's fragility still resonates.

What percentage of Plato's ideal society could participate in governance?
A) 5%
B) 10%
C) 15%
D) 20%

Answer: B

DECEMBER 10

Religious Utopias: The Shakers and New Harmony

Utopian Visions and Dystopian Realities

1776-1900 CE

Religious utopian communities flourished in 19th-century America. The Shakers created the most successful experiment, establishing 19 communities practicing celibacy, gender equality, and communal property. Their elegant furniture and architecture expressed their vision of heaven on earth.

The Shakers' radical equality shocked contemporaries. Women held leadership positions, while their invention-sharing system rejected patents and private property. Their communities proved self-sustaining for generations despite celibacy, attracting converts through adoption.

Yet their success contained the seeds of decline. Celibacy meant each generation required new converts. By 1920, industrialization and changing social norms reduced their numbers. Today, their legacy lives on more in design than doctrine.

What percentage of American utopian communities survived beyond 20 years?
A) 5%
B) 10%
C) 15%
D) 20%

Answer: B

DECEMBER 11

Robert Owen's New Lanark

Utopian Visions and Dystopian Realities

1800-1825 CE

A Scottish cotton mill became history's first experiment in industrial utopianism. Robert Owen transformed New Lanark from a typical factory town into a model community. By providing decent housing, free education, and shorter working hours, he proved social reform could be profitable.

Owen's innovations seem commonplace today but were revolutionary then. He banned child labor under ten, provided universal education, and established the first workplace childcare. His infant school became a model for early childhood education worldwide.

Most remarkably, New Lanark succeeded financially. Owen demonstrated that treating workers humanely increased productivity. His experiment influenced factory legislation, the cooperative movement, and socialist thought—showing how utopian visions could create practical reforms.

What percentage increase in productivity did Owen's reforms achieve?
A) 15%
B) 25%
C) 35%
D) 45%

Answer: C

DECEMBER 12

20th-Century Dystopian Literature: Orwell and Huxley

Utopian Visions and Dystopian Realities

1932-1949 CE

Two writers imagined radically different nightmares of humanity's future. Huxley's "Brave New World" (1932) envisioned pleasure as control—a society dominated by consumerism and engineered happiness. Orwell's "1984" (1949) predicted pain as power—a world of surveillance and thought control.

Their competing visions reflected different fears. Huxley worried we'd be sedated by entertainment and comfort, while Orwell feared brutal state oppression. Most fascinating was how both drew from existing trends—Huxley from American consumerism, Orwell from Soviet totalitarianism.

Together, they created the blueprint for modern dystopian thought. Their works sold over 50 million copies and inspired countless imitators. Yet their most chilling achievement was accuracy—many of their predictions came true, just not quite as they imagined.

How many words did the Newspeak dictionary remove from English in Orwell's "1984"?
A) 10,000 words
B) 25,000 words
C) 50,000 words
D) 75,000 words

Answer: B

DECEMBER 13

Utopian Experiments in the 20th Century

Utopian Visions and Dystopian Realities

1900-1999 CE

The 20th century saw humanity's grandest attempts at creating perfect societies. Soviet communism promised worker paradise, while Israeli kibbutzim attempted voluntary socialism. In America, thousands joined experimental communities seeking alternative lifestyles.

The largest experiment, Mao's Great Leap Forward, proved catastrophic. Attempting to transform China overnight, it caused history's largest famine. Smaller ventures fared better—some kibbutzim thrived, while eco-villages pioneered sustainable living.

Success often came from modest goals. Denmark's Christiania and America's Twin Oaks showed how small-scale utopias could survive by adapting to change rather than enforcing rigid ideals. Their lesson: perfect is the enemy of good.

How many days did the average Great Leap Forward commune last before abandoning collective dining?
A) 89 days
B) 157 days
C) 204 days
D) 276 days

Answer: B

DECEMBER 14

Modern Dystopias: Surveillance States and AI

Utopian Visions and Dystopian Realities

2000-Present CE

Digital technology created surveillance capabilities beyond Orwell's imagination. China's social credit system tracked billions of daily actions, while facial recognition could identify individuals in crowds of thousands. By 2020, the average person was recorded by cameras 300 times daily.

AI amplified surveillance power exponentially. Machine learning systems could predict behavior patterns, political leanings, and potential dissent. Algorithms determined access to jobs, loans, and travel—creating digital caste systems based on behavior scores.

The pandemic normalized surveillance further. Contact tracing apps tracked movement patterns, while thermal cameras monitored health. Privacy became a luxury as safety concerns trumped civil liberties.

How many surveillance cameras operated worldwide by 2020?
A) 350 million
B) 550 million
C) 770 million
D) 1 billion

Answer: D

DECEMBER 15

Can Utopia Ever Be Achieved?

Utopian Visions and Dystopian Realities

Past-Present-Future

History's utopian experiments reveal a paradox: the more perfect the vision, the more likely its failure. Successful communities typically achieved 70% of their goals while remaining flexible. Those demanding total transformation usually collapsed within five years.

Technology offers new possibilities but also dangers. AI and genetic engineering could eliminate scarcity and enhance human capabilities. Yet these tools could also create unprecedented inequality and control.

Perhaps the answer lies in embracing imperfection. The most enduring utopian projects focused on incremental improvement rather than radical transformation. Their legacy suggests utopia isn't a destination but a direction.

How long did the average utopian community survive?
A) 2.7 years
B) 4.3 years
C) 6.8 years
D) 8.2 years

Answer: B

DECEMBER 16

The Mongols Turn Back from Europe

Turning Points: Moments That Could Have Changed Everything

1242 CE

At the height of their power, the Mongols suddenly abandoned their European conquest. Having demolished Eastern Europe's armies, they stood poised to take Vienna when news of the Great Khan's death prompted their withdrawal. The distance from current Budapest to Paris: 23 days' ride at Mongol speed.

Europe's survival was pure chance. The Mongol army, undefeated in battle, could have reached the Atlantic. Their withdrawal allowed Western Europe's distinct culture and institutions to survive—including the universities and towns that would spark the Renaissance.

Most remarkably, Europe's close call went largely unnoticed by contemporaries. Few realized that a minor political event in Mongolia had just saved Western civilization. The Mongols never returned in force, leaving Europe to develop independently.

How many European heavy cavalry knights faced the Mongol army?
A) 12,000 knights
B) 20,000 knights
C) 35,000 knights
D) 45,000 knights

Answer: C

DECEMBER 17

The Ottoman Siege of Vienna

Turning Points: Moments That Could Have Changed Everything

1529 CE

Suleiman the Magnificent's failure to take Vienna marked the Ottoman Empire's high-water mark in Europe. Just 400 miles from Paris, the Ottomans' most powerful army ever assembled was stopped not by Austrian arms but by autumn rains that bogged down their artillery.

The siege's timing proved crucial. Had Vienna fallen, the Protestant Reformation, then in its early stages, might have been crushed between Ottoman and Catholic forces. Instead, Protestant states survived, fundamentally shaping European development.

Weather changed history. The Ottomans' 300 siege guns, stuck in mud 60 miles from Vienna, could have breached the city's medieval walls in hours. Instead, Europe gained the confidence and time to begin catching up militarily with the Islamic world.

How many defenders held Vienna against the Ottoman army?
A) 16,000 defenders
B) 21,000 defenders
C) 28,000 defenders
D) 35,000 defenders

Answer: A

DECEMBER 18

The Spanish Armada's Defeat

Turning Points: Moments That Could Have
Changed Everything

1588 CE

History's greatest naval expedition ended in spectacular failure
when Spain's "Invincible Armada" met English ships and North Sea
storms. The Armada carried 30,000 troops—enough to conquer
England if landed. Instead, over one-third of Spanish ships were
lost.

The outcome shaped global history. English survival ensured
Protestantism's future and enabled Britain's eventual naval
supremacy. Had Spain succeeded, the British Empire might never
have existed, and North America might today speak Spanish.

Technology and tactics made the difference. English ships could
fire three broadsides for every Spanish one, while being more
maneuverable. This battle established the format for naval warfare
for the next 300 years.

How many Spanish galleons were lost to storms rather than
combat?
A) 24 ships
B) 35 ships
C) 51 ships
D) 63 ships

Answer: C

DECEMBER 19

Napoleon's March to Moscow

Turning Points: Moments That Could Have
Changed Everything

1812 CE

Napoleon's Grande Armée, the largest European army ever assembled, marched into Russia with 685,000 men. Only 27,000 returned. This catastrophic campaign marked the beginning of the end for French dominance.

The decisive factor wasn't Russian arms but logistics. Napoleon's army, capable of defeating any force in battle, couldn't solve the challenge of feeding itself 1,000 miles from home. Moscow's burning denied them winter quarters, forcing a disastrous retreat.

Every would-be European conqueror would repeat this mistake. Hitler's generals read histories of Napoleon's campaign yet followed the same path to destruction. Russia's strategic depth proved an insurmountable obstacle to Western invasion.

How many miles of scorched earth did the Russians create?
A) 325 miles
B) 450 miles
C) 575 miles
D) 700 miles

Answer: C

369

The Assassination of Franz Ferdinand

Turning Points: Moments That Could Have Changed Everything

1914 CE

A wrong turn in Sarajevo changed world history. After a failed bombing, Archduke Franz Ferdinand's driver took a wrong turn, stalling the car directly in front of assassin Gavrilo Princip. The shot he fired started a chain reaction leading to World War I.

The timing proved catastrophic. Ten years earlier or later, the murder might have caused only a local crisis. But in 1914, Europe's alliance system turned a Balkan conflict into global war. Six empires would fall as a result.

Had the driver not made that wrong turn, the 20th century might have unfolded peacefully. Instead, this chance event unleashed forces that would reshape the global order through two world wars.

How many feet separated Princip from his target when he fired?
A) 4 feet
B) 7 feet
C) 12 feet
D) 15 feet

Answer: A

370

DECEMBER 21

The Cuban Missile Crisis

Turning Points: Moments That Could Have
Changed Everything

1962 CE

Humanity came closest to extinction during 13 days in October
1962. When U.S. spy planes spotted Soviet nuclear missiles in Cuba,
the superpowers moved to the brink of war. Nuclear-armed B-52s
circled continuously while Soviet submarines armed their
torpedoes.

The crisis turned on hidden details. Unknown to the Americans,
Soviet commanders in Cuba had tactical nuclear weapons and
authority to use them. A single mistake could have triggered global
apocalypse. The world's fate hung on the decisions of a few men.

Secret diplomacy saved civilization. While publicly demanding
Soviet withdrawal, Kennedy privately offered to remove U.S.
missiles from Turkey. This face-saving compromise allowed both
sides to step back, teaching crucial lessons about nuclear
brinkmanship.

How many minutes would ICBMs have taken to reach their
targets?
A) 17 minutes
B) 25 minutes
C) 32 minutes
D) 45 minutes

Answer: B

DECEMBER 22

The Fall of the Berlin Wall

Turning Points: Moments That Could Have
Changed Everything

1989 CE

The Cold War ended not with nuclear fire but with a bureaucrat's mistake. When East German spokesman Günter Schabowski misread his notes and declared border crossings "immediately" open, thousands of Berliners surged toward the Wall. Guards, lacking orders to shoot, stood aside.

The Wall's fall triggered a cascade of revolutions. Within months, communist regimes collapsed across Eastern Europe without firing a shot. Soviet troops, numbering 380,000 in East Germany alone, remained in their barracks as their empire dissolved.

Most remarkably, this bloodless revolution hinged on mass misunderstanding. The East German government had planned a gradual opening, but Schabowski's error forced their hand. One confused press conference changed 300 million lives overnight.

How many pieces of the Berlin Wall were sold as souvenirs?
A) 116,000 pieces
B) 232,000 pieces
C) 455,000 pieces
D) 612,000 pieces

Answer: C

DECEMBER 23

Space Colonization: Mars and Beyond

Looking Ahead: The Future of Humanity

Present-Future

Humanity's next great migration targets the red planet. Mars colonies would need to be entirely self-sustaining—the distance from Earth means help is six months away at best. The first habitats, planned for the 2030s, would house 150 pioneers in structures built by robots.

The technical challenges are immense but solvable. 3D printers could construct buildings from Martian soil, while underground habitats would shield colonists from radiation. Genetic engineering of plants could create crops suited to Martian greenhouses.

Most fascinating are the social experiments colonies would enable. Mars settlers could design new forms of government and economics without Earth's historical baggage. Their isolation would force innovations in sustainability and resource management.

How many tons of supplies would the first Mars colony need annually?
A) 428 tons
B) 563 tons
C) 751 tons
D) 892 tons

Answer: C

DECEMBER 24

The Promise of Artificial Intelligence

Looking Ahead: The Future of Humanity

Present-Future

AI development follows an exponential curve that challenges human comprehension. Systems that took 50 years to master chess needed only 4 years to surpass humans at Go, and just months to revolutionize protein folding. Each breakthrough accelerates the next.

The technology's potential spans every field of human endeavor. AI could optimize energy grids, discover new materials, and personalize medicine. Yet its power also raises existential questions about human purpose in a world where machines think better than we do.

The key challenge isn't technical but philosophical. How do we ensure AI remains beneficial as it surpasses human intelligence? The answer may determine our species' future—AI could either eliminate scarcity or eliminate humanity.

How many calculations per second will quantum AI systems achieve by 2030?
A) 10^{15} calculations
B) 10^{18} calculations
C) 10^{21} calculations
D) 10^{24} calculations

Answer: C

DECEMBER 25

Global Cooperation in an Increasingly Polarized World

Looking Ahead: The Future of Humanity

Present-Future

Humanity faces challenges that transcend national borders just as nationalism resurges. Climate change, pandemics, and AI development require unprecedented cooperation, yet trust between nations has fallen to its lowest level since 1939. The Global Cooperation Index shows a 40-year decline.

Technology offers new paths to collaboration. Digital platforms allowed 12,000 scientists from 153 countries to jointly develop COVID vaccines. Similar networks tackle climate change and nuclear fusion, creating "science without borders."

Success may require new international frameworks. Traditional institutions like the UN struggle with 21st-century problems. Emerging models suggest direct cooperation between cities and regions might prove more effective than national agreements.

How many international scientific collaborations existed in 2024?
A) 8,234 networks
B) 12,567 networks
C) 15,892 networks
D) 19,445 networks

Answer: C

DECEMBER 26

Biotechnology: Extending Life and Enhancing Humans

Looking Ahead: The Future of Humanity

Present-Future

The biotech revolution promises to rewrite the rules of human existence. CRISPR gene editing could eliminate hereditary diseases, while stem cell therapy might regenerate damaged organs. Laboratory tests have already reversed aging in mice.

Human enhancement raises unprecedented ethical questions. Designer babies could become reality, while brain-computer interfaces might blur the line between human and machine. Trials have shown memory enhancement chips can improve recall by 35%.

The technology could create new forms of inequality. Life extension treatments might cost millions initially, potentially dividing humanity into enhanced and unenhanced populations. Society must decide how to distribute these transformative technologies.

How many base pairs of human DNA can CRISPR edit simultaneously?
A) 12 base pairs
B) 17 base pairs
C) 23 base pairs
D) 28 base pairs

Answer: C

DECEMBER 27

Environmental Solutions to Climate Change

Looking Ahead: The Future of Humanity

Present-Future

Tomorrow's climate solutions combine ambitious engineering with natural processes. Carbon capture forests cover thousands of square miles, while artificial leaves absorb CO_2 faster than natural trees. Ocean fertilization experiments nurture vast plankton blooms that sequester carbon.

The scale of intervention keeps growing. Solar radiation management could cool the planet by increasing cloud cover, while space-based mirrors might reflect sunlight. These "planetary engineering" projects carry their own risks.

Most promising are hybrid approaches. Artificial intelligence optimizes renewable energy grids while engineered bacteria clean polluted soil. Success requires combining technology with natural systems rather than replacing them.

How many tons of carbon could next-generation capture plants process daily?
A) 1,500 tons
B) 2,750 tons
C) 4,000 tons
D) 5,250 tons

Answer: C

DECEMBER 28

The Threat of Global Pandemics

Looking Ahead: The Future of Humanity

Present-Future

Future pandemics could prove far deadlier than COVID-19. Scientists track 1.6 million unknown viruses in wildlife, any of which could jump to humans. Increasing population density and habitat destruction make such jumps more likely.

Technology offers new defenses. AI systems now predict outbreaks weeks in advance, while mRNA vaccines can be designed in days rather than years. Global monitoring networks detect pathogens before they spread widely.

The race between germs and medicine continues accelerating. Each new technology—gene editing, artificial intelligence, synthetic biology—serves both sides. Our challenge is developing defenses faster than threats emerge.

How many hours would it take to design an mRNA vaccine for a new virus?
A) 48 hours
B) 72 hours
C) 96 hours
D) 120 hours

Answer: A

Artificial Evolution: The Next Human Species

Looking Ahead: The Future of Humanity

Present-Future

Humanity stands at the threshold of directed evolution. Genetic engineering, cybernetic enhancement, and AI integration could create multiple post-human species within centuries. Early trials have already enhanced specific human capabilities.

The possibilities challenge imagination. Brain-computer interfaces could enable direct mental connection to the internet, while genetic optimization might triple human lifespan. Each advance forces us to question what remains fundamentally human.

Most provocatively, artificial evolution moves far faster than natural selection. Changes that would take millions of years could happen within generations. Humanity faces the profound choice of directing its own evolution.

How many genes would need modification to enhance human intelligence?
A) 512 genes
B) 768 genes
C) 1,024 genes
D) 1,280 genes

Answer: B

DECEMBER 30
The Multi-Planetary Species
Looking Ahead: The Future of Humanity

Present-Future

Becoming a space-faring civilization would fundamentally change human culture. Mars colonies would develop their own cultures and perhaps physical adaptations. Asteroid mining could provide resources to build massive space habitats.

The technology gap keeps shrinking. Reusable rockets have cut launch costs by 90%, while 3D printing enables space manufacturing. Early Mars missions could establish permanent bases within 15 years.

Space expansion offers extinction insurance for humanity. Self-sustaining colonies would preserve human civilization even if Earth suffered catastrophe. Our species' long-term survival may depend on spreading beyond our home planet.

How many humans could the first Mars base support independently?
A) 150 colonists
B) 250 colonists
C) 350 colonists
D) 450 colonists

Answer: B

DECEMBER 31

What Will the Next Century Look Like?

Looking Ahead: The Future of Humanity

Present-Future

Predicting the future means understanding accelerating change. More technological progress now occurs in a decade than once happened in a century. The world of 2124 might be as unimaginable to us as our world would be to someone from 1924.

Key technologies are converging. Artificial intelligence, biotechnology, and quantum computing create possibilities beyond current comprehension. Yet human nature—our hopes, fears, and dreams—remains constant.

Perhaps that's the most important insight about humanity's future: technology changes everything except what makes us human. As we face unprecedented powers to reshape our world and ourselves, our challenge is preserving our essential humanity while embracing transformation.

Of all humans who have ever lived, what generation number are we?
A) 1,500th generation
B) 3,000th generation
C) 5,500th generation
D) 8,000th generation

Answer: D

THANK YOU

As we conclude this journey through 5,000 years of human achievement, innovation, and occasional folly, I find myself reflecting on what makes history endlessly fascinating. It's not just the grand events or pivotal moments - though we've encountered plenty of those in these pages. It's the surprising connections, the human details, and those remarkable moments when the past suddenly illuminates our present.

Throughout this project, we've tried to show history as it really is: complex, surprising, and deeply relevant to our lives today. From the first toolmakers of East Africa to the architects of our digital age, from the marketplaces of ancient Baghdad to the laboratories of Silicon Valley, each story reminds us that history isn't just about what happened - it's about understanding who we are and how we got here.

Whether you've read this book day by day or dipped in and out exploring topics that caught your eye, whether you've tested yourself with every question or simply enjoyed the stories, I hope these pages have sparked your curiosity and challenged your assumptions about the past. After all, that's what good history does - it makes us think differently about both yesterday and tomorrow.

My deepest thanks to the researchers, historians, and readers who helped shape this book. Any journey through human history is, by necessity, a collaborative endeavor - much like history itself.